T0329189

Community-Oriented Education for Health Professionals:

A Cultural Analysis Approach to Curriculum Planning

Francis Sarr

Community-Oriented Education for Health Professionals:

A Cultural Analysis Approach to Curriculum Planning

Also by the author

Education for Community Health: Building a Community of Learning for the 21st *Century.* **(CENMEDRA 2017).**

Community-Oriented Education for Health Professionals:

A Cultural Analysis Approach to Curriculum Planning

Francis Sarr

Revised Edition

CENMEDRA

Published by CENMEDRA – the Centre for Media and Development Research in Africa

First published in The Gambia by Bohnjack Group Limited in 2013

This edition is published by CENMEDRA in 2018

www.cenmedra.org

ISBN: 978-9983-960-02-0

Front cover design by Sadibou Kamaso

Layout design by Folashade Lasisi JW

www.cenmedra.org

info@cenmedra.org

Contents

CHAPTER 1

Community Health and Population Health: A Comparative Analysis
The Realities
PHC Reforms
Summary

CHAPTER 2

Definition of the Curriculum Question
Educational Ideologies
Educational Focus on the Community
Summary

CHAPTER 3

The Subject-Centred Model
The Objectives Model
The Outcomes - Based Model
The Process Model
List of Worthwhile Activities
The Integrated Model
The Problem-Based Model
The Situational Analysis Model
Beattie's Fourfold Model
Summary

2. Technology, Community, and Information Exchange
3. Pedagogical, Curricular, and Co-curricular Design
Resistance to Organizational Change
Organisational Climate
Decision-making Process
Continuing Education
Resources
The Policy and Political Environment
Summary

Francis Sarr

List of Figures, Tables and Boxes

Figures:

1. Dahlgren and Whitehead Social Model of Health (1991)
2. Comparison of Traditional and Community Health-Oriented Nursing Practice
3. The Objectives Mode
4. Cultural Analysis Curriculum Planning Model
5. Phases of Learning in the Community

Tables:

1. Advantages and Disadvantages of the Subject-Centered Model
2. Advantages and Disadvantages of the Objectives Model
3. Advantages and Disadvantages of Outcome-Based Model
4. Advantages and Disadvantages of Process Model
5. Advantages and Disadvantages of the Integrated Model
6. Advantages and Disadvantages of the Problem-Based (PBL) Model
7. Advantages and Disadvantages of the Situated Analysis Model
8. Advantages and Disadvantages of Beattie's Fourfold Model
9. Existing Nursing School Subjects (Examples)
10. Comparison of Existing Nursing School Subjects (examples) with content required in Relation to the Eight Systems
11. Matrix A
12. Matrix B

Boxes:

1. Recommendations for Training and Education of Medical and Health Professional on the Social Determinants of Health
2. Key messages of the Marmot Report
3. Reasons for renewal of the Health-For-All Strategy
4. A Renewed PHC System: Five Areas for Action
5. List of Worthwhile Activities
6. Some Defining Features of PBL
7. The External and Internal Factors of the Situational Analysis Model
8. Sustainability: Five Fundamental Domains

Dedication

This book is dedicated to the entire family of Sangol and Tedene Sarr (my parents), particularly my late brother Moses Latirr Sarr who also loved writing, though in a field different from health – agricultural education – a subject he knew so well and was so passionate about, and liked to discuss with anyone who had the time and patience to listen to him.

About the author

Francis Sarr, Associate Professor of Community Health Education and Fellow of the West African College of Nursing, is the Dean of the School of Graduate Studies and Research of the University of The Gambia. He was educated at The Gambia School of Nursing and Midwifery (SRN Cert.); Pharmacy Department at The Gambia's Ministry of Health (Medical Aide Cert.); Cuttington University College, Liberia (BSc Nursing); University of Wales, Cardiff (M Ed, Curriculum Development & Educational Administration);  London University School of Hygiene and Tropical Medicine (MSc & Postgraduate Diploma, Public Health); London University Institute of Child Health (Nutrition & Child Health Cert.); and London South Bank University (PhD, Public Health).

He has a career in the health service that spans over a decade of working as a staff nurse and dispenser in urban and rural health services and 33 years of teaching in nursing and midwifery education. He participated in the planning of Primary Health Care (PHC) in The Gambia at headquarters and lower levels and was instrumental in the orientation of nursing and midwifery programmes to the PHC approach. A dedicated public health scholar and practitioner, Sarr is passionate about innovative approaches to healthcare education in the global South.

Acknowledgements

Several people who were helpful nationally and internationally in writing this book. Reviewers of the manuscript gave useful advice. They include Dr David Tembo, former WHO Representative in The Gambia, and Mrs Carolyn Mason, Associate Professor, Department of Nursing, Miami University, Ohio, USA. I am deeply grateful to them for their unfailing support. I wish to thank the many authors whose works I have cited, in particular Professor Denis Lawton, former Professor of Education and Deputy Director, University of London Institute of education, whose work *Curriculum Studies and Educational Planning* I relied on heavily. I also wish to express my gratitude to my friend Aloa Ahmed Alota for his advice and editorial support. I would also like to thank my family, especially my wife who has been my companion in my life's pursuits including writing a book. Finally, I wish to thank Dr Melvin George so much for writing the foreword.

About CENMEDRA

CENMEDRA – the Centre for Media and Development Research in Africa – is a knowledge centre. Registered as an educational charity in The Gambia on 3 March 2014 it aims to promote, facilitate and disseminate research in media, communication and development in Africa. Its activities are focused on five main areas namely media research, researching development, new media and society, education, and publication. In line with its underlying aim of research application, it shares its research results with policymakers, media and development practitioners, media houses, regulators, scholars, politicians, librarians, activists, donors, development agencies, and the wider research community. It has a two-tiered governance structure: a board of trustees drawn from the media, civil society and academia, which provides strategy and policy direction, and an administrative secretariat that is responsible for operations and policy implementation.

MISSION
CENMEDRA exists to foster innovative research that puts Africa on the path of peace, progress and prosperity.

VISION
CENMEDRA envisions an enlightened African society, free from the burden of ignorance, where everyone is able to realise their fullest potential in peace and prosperity.

VALUES
- Integrity
- Openness
- Creativity
- Diligence

Problems are solved by *thinking*, not by a special method.

"There is only one good – knowledge, and one evil – ignorance."
Socrates (circa 470-399BC)
http://www.cenmedra.org
Email: info@cenmedra.org

Foreword

The advent of Primary Health Care (PHC) as enshrined in the Alma-Ata Declaration and the adjoining principles created a new dimension and interest in community health. In response to the Declaration a number of programmes and interventions were implemented in pursuance of the said principles. The focus then was to create various categories of community health workers who presumably live and work within the communities and in this respect be more responsive to the needs and priorities of the communities.

Although a number of achievements have been made, some of the ideals of PHC are yet to be met; hence the commitment to PHC by member states of the World Health Organization to the PHC renewal principles of the World Health Report 2008 – Primary Health Care: now more than ever. Never in our current history has health been given so much prominence by world leaders and by communities as evidenced by the initiation of new multi-sectoral financing initiatives such as GAVI, Global Fund and Clinton Foundation, to name but a few. Communities likewise have also ensured and taken their rightful position in the governance structures of such initiatives. Having the numbers and quality of health workers at the right time and right places will go a long way in ensuring that current available resources are used efficiently and effectively to improve the health of communities.

Whilst numerous efforts have been initiated to produce various cadres of Community Health Workers (CHWs), not much energy has been put into the training of health professionals working in the community. These health professionals are not only supposed to be highly trained in the individual skills, but are also required to supervise and be involved in the training of CHWs and management of resources for and at the community level. Uncoordinated training of such professionals through individual curriculum is bound to send uncoordinated messages at the community level, thereby creating confusion and conflicting messages.

The value of this book therefore is that it has provided a framework for curriculum planning and made the argument for an integrated and interdisciplinary training of health professionals at the community level. The benefits of such an approach are immense given the fact that it is responsive to the socio-economic and cultural needs and demands of the community which are central to the health of the communities.

The book is recommended as a resource material to all health training institutions, teachers and students alike involved in curriculum development and teaching. It is also recommended to health professionals who may want to revisit the type of training and curriculum they want and thereby modifying their approach to working at the community level.

Dr Melville O. George*

(Dr Melville O. George was the Director of Health Services, The Gambia (1989-2005). He also served as Health Systems Adviser to the Malaria Unit/ WHO Regional Office for Africa, World Health Organization Representative to Ghana, Uganda and as Coordinator in the Global Health Workforce Alliance in WHO/Geneva)

Preface

There have been major shifts of emphasis over the years within the curriculum debate in health care. The debate goes back at least as far back as the 1940s. It focused on several issues including: (1) the great advances in medicine, science and public health in the last twenty-five years and the consequent need to reorient the training and practice of health workers, (2) the recognition that efficiency and effectiveness in health services required maximum functional capability output of all professional health workers and (3), the widening, theoretically and practically, of the education of health workers which had increased their competence (WHO 1986). But the real change came with the "Health for All" movement which was launched in 1977 with a resolution (WHA30. 43) adopted by the 30th World Health Assembly (WHO 1978). Consequently, the emphasis since then, perhaps especially in developing countries, has been the education and training of health personnel in the essentials of primary health care. This stress on primary health care as a major concentration of the curriculum debate has given rise to politico-economic forces, an evolution which is paralleled by a comparable change in the sociology of education for health professionals.

The factors that have seemingly made such a change unavoidable can be summarized into three main points. They are:(1) the pressures on schools to justify the use of public money on health professional education which is an unavoidable consequence of the recent economic recession in many countries, (2) the speed at which the process of social, technological and cultural changes occurs and (3) the ineffectiveness of educational systems to react properly to these changes and challenges.

In 2008, after more than 30 years of Primary Health Care (PHC) policy coming from the Alma Ata Declaration there has been calls for a renewal of PHC. For example, the World Health Report 2008 (WHO 2008) and the Report of the Commission on the Social Determinants of Health (Peters et al 2009) reaffirmed the relevance of PHC in terms of its vision and values in today's world. However, such calls for the renewal of the policy are not without commentary on the results. Member states of WHO agreed that with even 30 years of implementing PHC health systems still do not advance optimal care due to their failure to promote an appropriate balance in their efforts in terms of disease prevention, health promotion, cure and palliative care. Similarly, important challenges have been identified by others. For instance, in an article that reviews developments in the last 32 years and discusses the future of PHC policy Bhatia et al (2010) put forward three challenges for discussion. They are:

(i) the challenge of moving away from a narrow technical bio-medical para-digm of health to a broader social determinants approach and the need to dif-ferentiate primary care from primary health care; (ii) the challenge of tackling the equity implications of the market- oriented reforms and ensuring that the role of the State in the provision of welfare services is not further weakened; and (iii) the challenge of finding ways to develop local community commit-ments especially in terms of empowerment. They suggest that these challenges need to be addressed if PHC is to remain relevant in today's context, and con-clude that it is not sufficient to revitalize PHC of the Alma Ata Declaration but it must be reframed in light of the above discussion.

Such pressing challenges are characterized by enormously high complexity. Depending on past experience to decide what to do is no longer adequate. There is need to find new ways to solve problems that provide opportunities to discover innovations that have the potential to bring about a better and more promising future. The way we think and do things needs to change from close to open, from mere debating to reflective and generative dialogue, and from an autocratic leadership model to one of shared or collective leadership. But most importantly, there is need to have the will to change one's self before one can change the system. As managers of health care institutions and leaders to other health care providers, it is in the interest of health professionals (and others concerned), not only to take on these challenges, but also to get to grips with them- as far as their capabilities allow.

Unfortunately, many planners of educational programmes for health profes-sionals still use curriculum planning models that cannot adequately accommo-date the realities that account for the limitations in PHC and community-oriented education and practice. These realities, as Chapter1 shows, include especially social, political and economic factors, and other related factors that influenced health care in the past thirty-two years and will continue to do so now and in the future. Indeed, the Network of Community-oriented Institutions for the Health Sciences (Schmidt et al 1991), that was created at the instigation of WHO and whose main aim is to provide mutual support to member institu-tions that desire to adapt their curricula to the health needs of the communities they serve, has revealed that one of the lessons it has learnt in its ten years of existence is that "a more precise analysis of the political and socio-economic environments within which the schools operate is necessary...for achieving the desired goal of producing physicians who will contribute to the health of indi-viduals and communities. This is because in many countries the existing reali-ties of the healthcare delivery system significantly influence the ultimate per-formance of students, probably more than the types or quality of the education they receive in the schools. In fact, it was through analysis of the underlying social, economic and political causes of ill health that the report of the Commission on Social Determinants of Health (Peters et al 2009) made a case for and supported the renewal of the PHC policy. Thus, from a health professional education perspective, one can draw strong justification from these and many similar experiences for providing the health professional opportunities for understanding of such realities in healthcare and developing the skills necessary to deal with them with the aim to enhance the PHC policy.

This book advocates a cultural analysis approach to planning health professional education for community health- an education in which, alongside other prominent skills, the graduates behave in a caring manner. It is a method by which course planners can analyse the culture of a society- the social (including health), economic, communication, rationality, technology, morality, belief and aesthetic systems of culture (Lawton (1983) - to obtain a clear picture of the factors health professionals confront. Course planners can improve existing educational programmes, or develop new programmes that are more relevant to community health needs, by using a cultural analysis approach in curriculum development. Educational models, principles and scenarios are offered to guide course planners, policy makers and other stakeholders in related curriculum planning processes. The cultural analysis curriculum planning approach proposed in this book is, firstly, a method of education and is therefore applicable to planning education for all health professionals- doctors, nurses, dentist, etc, trained persons who help in identifying or preventing or treating illness or disability. Secondly, based on a wider view of education, it is flexible and open enough to accommodate important educational proposals in community health, such as interdisciplinary education. If the success required in this and other important areas of learning is to be achieved, the educational needs that health professionals have in common must be planned together by curriculum planners in the different health professions. Thus, the emphasis throughout this text is on concepts like common curriculum, integrated learning, interdisciplinary learning, student-centred learning and other progressive approaches to education.

In this book community-oriented education for health professionals means education that incorporates the principles and elements of Primary health care, community health and population health, although the term community health is mostly used. Thus, the programmes that provide such education consider (Schmidt et al 1991) the major health problems of a country where graduates of the programmes function. This means that, firstly, the content of the programmes is not only based on the discipline that contributes to them, but also on the problems that characterize the programmes. Secondly, the particular character of the major health problems in a specific population differentiates one programme from another. Thirdly, because problems change from time to time, programmes are highly oriented to changes in the environment. Finally, the student activities in the programmes should include issues in health education and promotion, disease prevention, health research and Involvement of people in improvement of their health status.

The organizing scheme of this book clearly shows its unique approach. The book is divided into ten chapters. Chapter 1 discusses the concepts, principles and elements of Primary Health Care, Community Health and Population Health, the factors that were pivotal to the development of PHC as well as PHC reforms. Chapter 2 firstly explains the curriculum question by looking at the two broad approaches to the meaning of the term curriculum in order to understand its relevance to the thrust of this book. Then it examines some educational ideologies that underline the different definitions of the term curriculum. Finally, the chapter looks at the necessary changes in the curriculum of health professionals that PHC and Community/Population Health demand. Chapter 3 describes curriculum planning models in the literature that are used in health professional education. The models occur in two main categories, prescriptive and descriptive curriculum models, reflecting the two main approaches to defining the meaning of curriculum. Chapter 4 firstly clarifies the meaning of the terms culture and cultural analysis which are highly relevant if the cultural analysis approach is to be fully understood. It then describes the cultural analysis model including its eight interrelated systems, which according to Lawton (1993), make up a society's culture. In Chapter 5 the application of the cultural analysis framework is considered by viewing society in terms of the eight systems of culture already described in Chapter 4. Chapter 6 considers the selection from the eight systems of culture by looking at the degree to which the eight systems should be covered by present subjects, and suggests the quality and appropriateness of such coverage in health professional education for the community. The context of curriculum planning is covered in Chapter 7. Here, the focus is on the influences and constraints outside as well as inside education that operate on curriculum planning, including how the evaluation system affects curriculum planning and curriculum innovation and change. Chapter 8 deals with the issue of covering the subject-matter or ground of the common curriculum adequately. Chapter 9 considers issues concerning how to organise the common curriculum on the basis of cultural analysis conducted in the previous stages taking into consideration important educational strategies and procedures and psychological theories and questions that have a bearing on teaching and learning. The final chapter, Chapter 10, considers how to manage the curriculum innovation and change with particular reference to the will or purposes of teachers and their collaborators in curriculum planning. In doing so, several of the conceptual and operative constraints of curriculum planning and the implementation of curriculum innovation and change outlined in Chapter 7 are discussed.

The ideas in these chapters are not a plan for reconstructing the educational order, or a remedy for all ills. However, they advise approaches that can facilitate the more determined educational reforms that are required to better educate health professionals for roles in the community now and in the future.

Francis Sarr

1

The Concepts, Principles and Elements of Community Health, Population Health and Primary Health Care

Community Health and Population Health: A Comparative Analysis

Community means a group of people who live in a defined geographical location and are governed by the same rules and regulations, norms, values, goals and organisation. Its members are committed to interacting with one another broadly and honestly (Scott Peck 1993). It can set standards for members and create the environment for great achievements (Manning *et al* 1996)

The term community health means the health status of a defined group of people or community and the actions and conditions that protect and improve the health of the community (Green *et al* 2002). For instance, the health status of people living in a particular village and the actions taken to protect and improve their health constitutes community health. However, in addition to communities there are other groups that frequently need health care and are of relevance to policymakers. Therefore, the term population health has been proposed (Green *et al* 2002). However, according to Kindig *et al* (2003p1), this term is relatively new and has not been properly defined. They therefore propose this definition of population health: "The health outcomes of a group of individuals, including the distribution of such outcomes within the group." Kindig *et al* argue that the field of population health should include patterns of health determinants and health outcomes as well as policies and interventions that connect health determinants and health outcomes. Determinants of health include medical care systems (e.g., resource allocation and health interventions), the social environment (e.g., income, education and social support) and the physical surroundings (e.g., clean air and water, and urban design). Examples of health outcomes are longevity and health-related quality of life.

The term population health is similar to community health. The difference between population health and community health lies only in the scope of the people dealt with or the degree of organization (McKenzie *et al* 2011). The health statuses of populations who are not organized or have no identity as a group or locality and the actions and conditions needed to protect and improve the health of these populations constitute population health (McKenzie *et al* 2011). Examples of populations are women over fifty years, adolescents, and adults between twenty-five and forty-four years of age, seniors living in public housing, prisoners, and blue-collar workers. It is clear from these examples that a population could be a segment of a community, a category of people in several communities of a region, or workers in various industries. The reader is referred to the wealth of literature around community and population for further exploration of the terms and concepts. Examples are Ruderman, M (2000) and Green *et al* (1999).

As health is influenced by a wide array of socio-demographic factors, relevant variables range from the proportion of residents of a given age group to the overall life expectancy of the neighbourhood. Medical interventions designed to improve the health of a community range from improving access to medical care to public health communications campaigns (Green *et al* 2012).

Currently, community health studies are focusing on how the built environment and socio-economic status affect community/population health. This is because there is growing evidence to show, for example, that physical and mental problems are linked to the built environment, including human places like homes, schools, workplaces and industrial areas (Srinivasan *et al* 2003). Such a research concentration is particularly relevant to educating health professionals in the community because it deals with the surroundings created by human beings for learning, such as buildings and neighbourhoods and their supporting infrastructure (e.g., water supply or energy networks). The built environment is a material, spatial and cultural product of human labour that combines physical elements and energy in forms suitable for living, working and playing. Practically, the built environment refers to the interdisciplinary field which addresses the design, construction, management and use of these man-made surroundings as an interrelated whole as well as their relationship to human activities over time. The discipline draws upon areas such as economics, law, public policy, management, geography, design, technology, and environmental sustainability (Chynoweth 2006). The following paragraphs show why and how this relates to community/population health.

As the WHO also suggests: The social conditions in which people live powerfully influence their chances to be healthy. Indeed factors such as poverty, social exclusion and discrimination, poor housing, unhealthy early childhood conditions and low occupational status are important determinants of most diseases, deaths and health inequalities between and within countries (WHO 2004, as cited by Dahlgren *et al* 1991).

Let us use the Dahlgren and Whitehead (1991) Social Model of Health Figure 1) to help explain the layers of influence on community/population health and discuss inequalities in health based on socioeconomic position. In discussing the layers of influence on health, Dahlgren and Whitehead (1991) outline a social ecological theory to health. They try to map the relationship between individuals, their environment and disease.

Figure 1: Dahlgren and Whitehead Social Model of Health (1991)

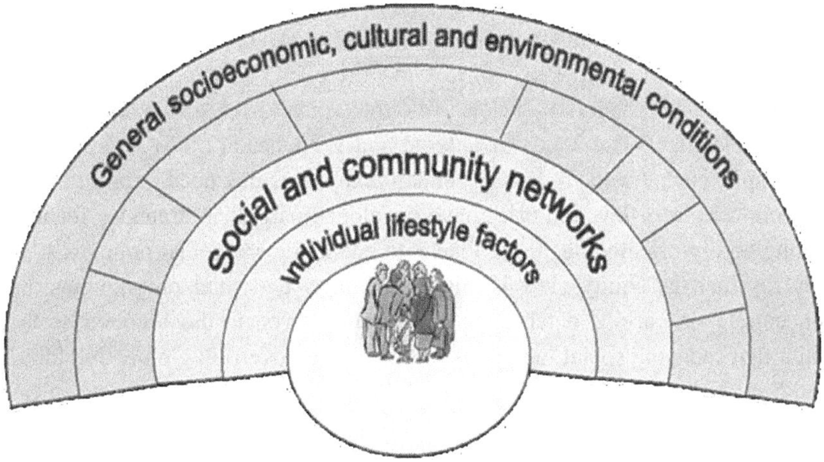

Source: Dahlgren and Whitehead (1991)

The model shows the following influences on community/population health:

1. **At the centre** are individuals with a set of fixed genes. They are surrounded by influences on health that can be changed.
2. **First layer** is personal behaviour and lifestyle. These can promote or damage health, for example, choosing to drink alcohol or not. Here, individuals are affected by friendship patterns and the norms of their community.
3. **Second layer** is social and community influences, which provide mutual support for members of the community in unfavourable conditions. But they can also fail to provide support or have a negative effect.
4. **Third layer** includes structural factors, namely housing, working conditions, access to services and provision of essential facilities.

The model provides a useful framework for inquiring about the largeness of the contributions of each of the layers to health; the possibility of converting particular factors and the reciprocal actions needed to induce connected factors in other layers. Also, the model can be used for constructing several hypotheses on the inter-working between the different determinants of health, and the comparative influences of those determinants on various determinants (Public Health Action Support Group 2011). In the introduction of their work entitled *European Strategies for Tackling Social Inequities in health,* Dahlgren and Whitehead (2006) point to this relationship between the individual, his or her environment and disease, and the unfairness of health inequities, which they say are caused by unhealthy public policies and lifestyles influenced by structural factors. They highlight the importance given to efforts at reducing health inequities by an increasing number of countries and international bodies, such as some European Union countries and WHO, and the importance of improving health generally, especially in low-income countries, through attempts by countries and international agencies like the Commission on Social Determinants of Health (WHO 2008). Dahlgren and Whitehead (2006) also point out that despite such efforts, there still remain many gaps that need to be filled. As they indicate, very few countries have developed particular strategies for integrating equity-oriented health policies into economic and social policies. Also, they say that the equity view is missing in many particular programmes that concentrate on various determinants of health, "even in those countries that claim that reducing social inequities in health is an overriding objective for all health-related policies and programmes". They further suggest that when one considers that people see health as composing one of the most significant dimensions of their welfare, the low priority it is accorded is disproportionate to its significance.

It is worth focusing further on the Commission on Social Determinants of Health (WHO 2008) as its recommendations, particularly those on education and training, have much relevance for community-oriented education for health professionals. The Commission on Social Determinants of Health was set up by the WHO in 2005 to arrange the evidence on what can be done to promote health equity, and to foster a global movement to achieve it. The Commission identified three principles of action which are included in three overarching recommendations, which WHO sees as critical for achieving a more equitable and highest attainable standard of health. The three main principles are:

- Improve daily living conditions
- Tackle the inequitable distribution of power and money
- Measure and understand the problem and assess the impact of action

Box 1 presents the Commission's recommendations for training and education of medical and health professionals on the social determinants of health that are linked to the above three main recommendations.

> **Box 1: Recommendations for Training and Education of Medical and Health Professionals on the Social Determinants of Health**
>
> - Educational institutions and relevant ministries make the social determinants of health a standard and compulsory part of training of medical and health professionals.
> - The healthcare sector has an important stewardship role in inter-sectoral action for health equity.
> - The recommended reorientation of the healthcare sector towards a greater importance of prevention and health promotion.
> - Making the social determinants of health a standard and compulsory part of medical training and training of other health professionals requires that textbooks and teaching materials are developed for this purpose.

Source: WHO (2008)

The WHO (2008) offers several specific curriculum proposals on training and education of medical and health professionals on the social determinants of health together with the above recommendations:

- Medical and health professionals should be aware of health inequities as an important public health problem, and understand the importance of social factors in influencing the level and distribution of population health.
- Policymakers and professionals in the healthcare sector should understand how social determinants influence health, and how the healthcare sector, depending on its structure, operations, and financing, can exacerbate or ameliorate health inequities.
- Medical and health professionals need to be aware of how gender influences health outcomes and health-seeking behaviour.
- There should be reorientation in the skills, knowledge, and experience of the health personnel involved in disease prevention and health promotion and an enhancement of the professional status and importance of these areas.
- Textbooks and teaching materials should be developed for the purpose of making the social determinants of health a standard and compulsory part of medical training and training of other health professionals. This includes an urgent need to develop, among other things, a virtual repository of teaching and training materials on a broad range of social determinants of health that can be downloaded without cost.
- Opportunities for interdisciplinary professional training and research on social determinants of health should be created. For low-income countries, the creation of such training and education opportunities can happen, for example, through regional centres of learning and/or distance education models.

Like the WHO Report of the Commission on the Social Determinants of Health (WHO 2008), the Marmort Report (UCL Institute of Health Equity 2010), entitled *Fair Society, Healthy Lives*, focuses on proposing the most effective evidence-based strategies for reducing health inequalities, in this case in England from 2010. In doing so the report does a number of things:

- It proposes an evidence- based strategy to address the social determinants of health, the conditions in which people are born, grow, live, work and age and which can lead to health inequalities.
- It draws further attention to the evidence that most people in England are not living as long as the best off in society and spend longer in ill health. Preventable illnesses and premature death affect everyone below the top.
- It proposes a new way to reduce health inequalities in England post-2010.
- It argues that, traditionally, government policies have focused resources only on some segments of society. To improve health for all and to reduce unfair and unjust inequalities in health, action is needed across the social gradient.

Box 2 presents the key messages of the Marmot Report:

Box 2: Key Messages of The Marmot Report

1. Reducing health inequalities is a matter of fairness and social justice. In England, the many people who are currently dying prematurely each year as a result of health inequalities would otherwise have enjoyed, in total, between 1.3 and 2.5 million extra years of life.
2. There is a social gradient in health – the lower a person's social position, the worse his or her health.
3. Health inequalities result from social inequalities. Action on health inequalities requires action across all the social determinants of health.
4. Focusing solely on the most disadvantaged will not reduce health inequalities sufficiently. To reduce the steepness of the social gradient in health, actions must be universal, but with a scale and intensity that is proportionate to the level of disadvantage.
5. Action taken to reduce health inequalities will benefit society in many ways. It will have economic benefits in reducing losses from illness associated with health inequalities. These currently account for productivity losses, reduced tax revenue, higher welfare payments and increased treatment costs.
6. Economic growth is not the most important measure of our country's success. The fair distribution of health, well-being and sustainability are important social goals. Tackling social inequalities in health and tackling climate change must go together.
7. Reducing health inequalities will require action on six policy objectives:
   - Give every child the best possible start in life.
   - Enable all children, young people and adults to maximise their capabilities

---

and have control over their lives.

- Create fair employment and good work for all.
- Ensure healthy standard of living for all.
- Create and develop healthy and sustainable places and communities.
- Strengthen the role and impact of ill-health prevention.

8. Delivering these policy objectives will require action by central and local government, the National Health Service (NHS), the private sectors and community groups. National policies will not work without effective local delivery systems focused on health equity in all policies.

9. Effective local delivery requires effective participatory decision-making at local level. This can only happen by empowering individuals and local communities.

Source: UCL Institute of Health Equity (2014)

As will be seen, many of these proposals, particularly those of the WHO Report of the Commission on the Social Determinants concerning training and education, are consistent with the major parts of this book, especially Chapters 2, 6 and 10 on the curriculum, educational ideologies and educational focus on the community, a selection from culture, and managing the curriculum innovation and change, respectively. The frameworks that these chapters offer can assist community health educators who want to reorient the skills, knowledge, and experiences of community health personnel on the social determinants of health and enhance learning in community.

We must now consider the concept of PHC which is closely related to the idea of community/population health and education of health professionals for the community.

Principles and Elements of Primary Health Care

Community health mainly in the contexts of developing countries is usually studied and delivered based on the PHC approach (e.g. Golladan (1980). Community health services play an important role in the primary health care system and aim to improve the health and well-being of people, especially people who are at risk of poorer health. Community health services provide a strong stage for the delivery of a range of primary health care services, such as child health services. If delivered effectively, a PHC system can improve the health of a population and reduce inequalities in health care (Department of Health 2014), which has been the focus of much of the foregoing discussion.

Members of the 13th World Health Assembly committed themselves to the PHC approach by adopting the resolution of "Health for All by the Year 2000" and define PHC thus:

...essential health care based on practical, scientifically sound and so-cially accepted methods and technology made universally accessible to individuals and families in the community through their full participation and at a cost that the community and country can afford to maintain at every stage of their development in the spirit of self-reliance and self-determination (WHO1978: 6).

The principles of PHC have been simplified thus: the health care services should be accessible to all; there should be maximum individual and com-munity involvement in the planning and operation of health care services; the focus of care should be on prevention and promotion rather than on cure; appropriate technology should be used – that is, methods, procedures, techniques and equipment should be scientifically valid, adapted to local needs and acceptable to users and to those for whom they are used; health care is regarded as only a part of total health development - other sectors such as education, housing, nutrition are all essential for the attainment of a person's well-being.

Within the limits of this outline are eight important elements of a PHC ser-vice:

- Education on common health problems and ways to control and prevent them.
- Appropriate nutrition and improvement of food provision.
- Safe water supply and basic sanitation.
- Health care for mothers and children, incorporating family planning.
- Immunization towards the main infectious diseases.
- Prevention and control of locally endemic diseases.
- Proper treatment of prevalent injuries and diseases.
- Supply of essential drugs (WHO 1978)

A PHC approach places emphasis on community-based services with in-creased attention to early intervention and prevention strategies such as health promotion. To be successful, community health programmes must depend on the dissemination of information by health professionals to the general public, using mass communication (one-to-one or one-to-many communication). Moreover, there is now a growing move towards health marketing (processes for creating, communicating, delivering, and exchanging offerings that have value for customers, clients, partners, and society at large) that combines tradi-tional marketing principles and theories together with science-based strategies to prevention, health promotion and health protection (CDC 2011). Let us now look at the factors that contributed to the development of PHC in the past three decades.

Francis Sarr

The Realities

The effects of the dramatic social, political and economic changes such as liberal democratic systems, which came after the end of the Cold War and remained during the last ten years of the twentieth century, will continue to influence the daily lives of people globally in the 21st century in several ways. There will be continuous demands for social justice and respect for human rights, good governance, democracy, and a clear definition of the role of the state (WHO 1995). There will be enduring calls for the expansion of the involvement of communities in economic globalisation and decision-making (WHO 1995). Also, frequently there will be a need to adapt and change planned economies to market economies. Although the advantages of these changes are still unquestionable, clearly many countries are unable to make them in the medium-term due to socio-economic constraints and other factors.

The burden on governments to meet competing political, social and economic demands often results in the adoption of short-term reforms, which are usually far less effective (WHO 1995). In consequence, the drive towards immediate increased economic efficiency often leads to a reduction of funds for social programmes, in particular health care programmes (WHO1995). Although in many countries per capital income has increased in the last 40 years, many people are yet to experience improvements in quality of life, and many have suffered as a result of the changed processes (Shah 2013). For example, because of the structural adjustment policies of the World Bank and the International Monetary Fund (IMF), national governments are finding it increasingly difficult to ensure that their people get health care, food and education, which are basic human rights. Many developing countries have experienced deepening poverty and crippling debts as a result of such policies. Scores of people have been displaced, or are refugees; burdened or disadvantaged by unrestrained exploitation and war. War in turn has caused resource diversion and ruin in many parts of the world.

Several factors aggravate this situation in which governments are striving to meet competing social, economic and political demands. There is an increase in the total world population with the resultant pressure on health services. Additionally, not only has the number of poor people doubled in the last 15-20 years; but the gap between literate and illiterate people, rich and poor, in developed and developing nations is expanding (WHO 1995). This is seen more so in developing than in developed countries. During the 1960s, the income of 20 percent of the richest segment of the world's population was 30 times more than a similar number of the poorest segment (WHO 1995).This difference in income doubled in the 1990s. Moreover, the average consumption rate of natural resources in developed countries is 10-12 times that consumed by developing nations (WHO 1995). This widening gap between the rich and the poor, who cannot gain technology for development, represents the fundamental differences in today's world (Jeguier 1981).

The massive capital movement from industrialized countries to poor ones goes to countries with the capacity to provide large markets and export industrial material (WHO 1995). This is mainly due to private investment. Despite the important role technical cooperation and external aid play, the volume of bilateral assistance to the health sectors of poor countries has been dwindling. Government measures and economic adjustment programmes have proved to be ineffective alternatives for health development. Therefore, it is imperative that donors earmark adequate resources and other necessary requirements for sustainable development, poverty alleviation, relief and conflict resolution (WHO 1995).

It is clear from what is portrayed above that economic, political, environmental, social, and cultural factors were instrumental in the development of PHC in the past three decades. As information from the 1994 monitoring of the Health-for-All Strategy (cited in WHO1995) also indicates, these influences will remain the major determinants of health in the 21st century. These factors not only constitute the background for change that was formally expressed in 1978 at Alma-Ata; they also form the basis for the renewal of the Health-for-All Strategy (WHO 2014).

Box 3 provides reasons given by the WHO for the renewal of the Health – for - All Strategy that reflects very much the social, economic, environmental and political realities described above.

Box 3: Reasons for renewal of the Health – for - All Strategy

Why a renewal of primary health care (PHC), and why now, more than ever? The immediate answer is the palpable demand for it from Member States – not just from health professionals, but from the political arena as well.

Globalisation is putting the social cohesion of many countries under stress, and health systems, as key constituents of the architecture of contemporary societies, are clearly not performing as well as they could and as they should.

People are increasingly impatient with the inability of health services to deliver levels of national coverage that meet stated demands and changing needs, and with their failure to provide services in ways that correspond to their expectations. Few would disagree that health systems need to respond better – and faster – to the challenges of a changing world. PHC can do that.

Source: WHO (2014)

However, what are the implications of pursuing this direction for health professional education in the 21st century? We will consider this question in Chapter 2 by looking at the proposed changes in curricula required for primary health care and community health. In the next section, we will consider important PHC reforms since the initiation of the PHC approach.

PHC Reforms

Primary health care reforms have been discussed and proposed in many different countries since members of the 13th World Assembly adopted the resolution of "Health for All by the Year 2000". The expectations of Health-for-All had led countries to formulate different models of health care towards such a goal during recent decades, creating opportunities that have stimulated a series of new health concepts and paradigms. In The Gambia, for example, PHC was adopted in 1979 as the basis for the provision of essential health care and became an integral component of development programmes.

The PHC approach in The Gambia aimed at mobilizing all potential resources, including the communities' own resources, towards the development of a national health care system. The intention was to extend health service coverage to the entire Gambian population and to tackle the main disease problems of their communities. PHC is also a mechanism for guaranteeing an equitable re-distribution of the limited health resources available in the country in favour of the underserved majority who live and work in rural areas (MOH 1981).

There are many conceptions on which the principles and concepts of PHC are based (e.g. Bhatia *et al* 2010). One such example is the conceptualization of Community-based Integrated Care (Plochg *et al* 2002), which features a health system that is based upon and driven by community health needs. Moreover, it is tailored to the health beliefs, preferences, and societal values of that community and assures a certain level of community participation. Recently, this approach was renewed by introducing terms such as responsiveness and stewardship. Another example is Community-Oriented Primary Care, defined as a "continuous process by which primary health care is provided to a defined community on the basis of its assessed health needs through the planned integration of public health practice with the delivery of primary health care" (Mullan *et al* 2002, p 1748). Mullan *et al* provide a global overview of COPC, tracing its conceptual roots, reviewing its many manifestations, and exploring its prospects as an organizational paradigm for the democratic organization of community health services. They examine the pitfalls and paradoxes of the concept and suggest its future utility.

A main belief of the renewed push for PHC, as suggested by Gofin *et al* (2005), is that community medicine and primary health care are actually a component of a unified practice, pointing out the relationships between PHC and community-oriented primary care (COPC): a comprehensive approach that identifies health needs or problems; taking into account socio-economic and cultural factors that determine health, and providing healthcare to a whole community. While these conceptions of health care may vary somewhat in their meanings, what they all clearly have in common is the emphasis that the concepts of PHC should be integrated into the practice of community health care in homes, dispensaries, health centres and hospitals, which constitute the different levels of health care.

Most definitions of PHC in relation to a renewed primary health care system would have the following characteristics:

More community-based PHC organizations focus on the specific needs of the individuals and populations that they serve.

Greater coordination and integration with other health services, for example, hospitals and home care services.

A greater emphasis on health promotion, illness and injury prevention and the management of chronic diseases, to help people stay healthy and not just focus on treatment once they are sick.

Care provided by a team of primary health care providers (for example, nurses, family, physicians, nutritionists, counsellors, just to name a few) so that the most appropriate care is provided by the most appropriate provider.

Greater access to health services, on a 24/7 basis, so that people can get advice and care outside of regular office hours.

In order to meet the requirements of 'a renewed primary health care system' professionals will be required to collaborate to develop comprehensive care plans (e.g. WHO 2014). This will require professionals to take the time to get to know the skills that different professional groups bring to the PHC setting. Not only will PHC teams be challenged to incorporate various approaches through which to see clients, they will also be challenged to develop an understanding of, and responsiveness to, the changing needs of the communities they serve.

On a more macro level, a genuine PHC approach will require governments to take into account the physical, social and economic factors that impact upon individuals and shift the focus away from treating illness to broader social health focus to tackle inequalities in health. The World Health Organization has identified five areas for action (Box 4):

Box 4: A Renewed PHC System: Five Areas for Action

- build healthy public social policy
- create supportive environments
- strengthen community action
- re-orient health services
- develop individual personal skills

Source: WHO (1987)

One of the challenges posed by Bhatia *et al* (2010), for example, concerning the renewed push for PHC is moving away from a narrow technical bio-medical paradigm of health to a broader social determinants approach and the need to differentiate primary care from primary health care. The difference between the meaning and the appropriate use of the concepts of "primary health care" and "primary care" has been further explained by, for instance, the Report of the Canadian National Primary Health Care Conference (Lewis *et al* 2004). According to the report, primary care deals mainly with the prevention and treatment of sickness. It is what many people think of as front-line care. Conventionally, this takes the form of a visit to the family doctor. Primary care may involve preventative activities, immunization, diagnosis and treatment of illness. However, such care does not usually include a comprehensive, inter-sectional approach to producing or enhancing health. Perhaps most crucially, primary care concentrates on individuals and families, but not the community as the unit of intervention which, as we have seen in the explanation above, is one of the hallmarks of the primary health care approach. Nevertheless, prima-ry care is an essential subset of primary health care. They are complementary, and neither can be effective or efficient without the other. Thus, the idea of education for community health, as used in this book, incorporates both con-ceptions of primary care and primary health care.

Summary

This chapter has looked at the concepts, principles and elements of commu-nity health and the primary health care approach on which the implementation of community health in the developing country context is usually based. Also, the chapter has considered the factors that were pivotal to the development of PHC, as well as important PHC reforms. Community health is a discipline that deals with the health status of a defined and organized group of people, or community, and the actions and conditions that protect and improve the health of the community. A similar concept, population health, means the health sta-tus of populations who are not organized or have no identity as a group or lo-cality and the actions and conditions needed to protect and improve the health of these populations. Community health mainly in developing countries is usu-ally delivered based on the PHC approach. Many healthcare concepts rest on the principles and ideas of PHC and Community Health. For example, there is the idea of Community-based Integrated Care, which features a health system that is based upon and driven by community health needs.

However, much more than policy statements and dedicated resources are required to advance the needed shift in thinking away from institutional models and the emphasis on the treatment of illness. To meet the needs of 'a renewed primary health care system' professionals will, for instance, be required to col-laborate to develop comprehensive care plans. There are several challenges on the renewed push for PHC, such as moving away from a narrow technical biomedical paradigm of health to a broader social determinants approach and the need to differentiate primary care from primary health care. These two concepts are, however, reciprocal and are required for an efficient PHC/Community Health education system.

Whatever the health profession, the point is that any course in PHC/Community health education incorporating a substantial cultural component will require a distinctive planning model: a culture analysis planning model. The decision to have teachers plan curricula by cultural analysis will have many implications for course development. Later chapters will consider the issues in curriculum planning which are brought out by a curriculum planning approach through cultural analysis. But for one to appreciate the value of this curriculum planning option in the context of community-oriented education for health professionals, it is necessary to comprehend the thinking on the meaning of the term curriculum and the different ideologies that underline the different definitions of curriculum, and views on which the evolution and use of commonly employed curriculum planning models in health care are based, together with their implications for the practice of health professionals and ways they must be prepared for such practice. The following chapter begins with the definition of the term curriculum, it then discusses some educational ideologies and finally looks at the proposed changes in the focus of the curriculum that are required by primary health care and community/population health.

2

The Curriculum, Educational Ideologies and Educational Focus on the Community

This chapter will firstly explain the curriculum question by looking at the two broad approaches to the meaning of the term curriculum in order to understand its relevance to the thrust of this book. Then it will examine some educational ideologies that underline the different definitions of the term curriculum. Finally, the chapter will look at the proposed changes in the focus of the curriculum that primary health care and community and population health demand.

Definition of the Curriculum Question

There are two contrasting interpretations of the term curriculum. Some scholars view it as the *content* of a particular subject area of study. This narrow definition of curriculum is often compared with the broader meaning which includes not only *content*, but also *how* and *why* a subject area is taught. Some view the curriculum as a direct *intention*, a *prescription,* or *plan*, for example, a book of instructions for teachers. Others view curriculum as *what* actually happens in schools as a consequence of teachers' activities, for example, the performance or achievement of schools. The aim of curriculum study is to connect these two perspectives of curriculum as intention and as a reality (Stenhouse 1975). The major problem of connecting intention with reality is the gap between our ideas and ambitions and the efforts at making them operative. In order to address issues such as content and its justification, the translations of plans, etc, one should draw on aspects of sociology, psychology, history and philosophy. It is for this reason that the term curriculum is often seen as the means by which the experience of attempting to put an educational proposal into practice is made publicly available. It involves both content and method, and when applied broadly it considers the problem of implementation in the institutions it is used.

This idea of curriculum is popular apparently due to the fact that it is more encompassing, as it includes both content and method. Hence, it is seen to be more practical in dealing with the curriculum question. It resembles the four ways of approaching curriculum theory and practice (Infed 2010): curriculum as a body of knowledge to be transmitted, curriculum as a means for realizing particular ends in students, product, curriculum as a process, and curriculum as praxis. The idea of curriculum as praxis is in many ways a development of the curriculum process model (Chapter 3), but unlike the curriculum process model, it makes clear statements about the interests it serves: it makes continuous reference to collective human well-being and the freedom of the human spirit. This offer is helpful to consider in approaching curriculum theory and practice in the light of Aristotle's influential classification of knowledge into three disciplines-theoretical, productive and practical (Infed 2010).

This approach, as we shall see later in the following chapters, agrees with the application of cultural analysis in curriculum planning, the focus of this book. When applied to curriculum planning, the cultural analysis approach takes into consideration, among other things, the nature, values, development and dynamics of society and in what ways they influence learning and the learner. This makes appropriate for planning community-oriented education and training for health professionals.

Educational Ideologies

Educators have various value systems which form the basis of the way they develop curriculum. It is important to understand that the ideologies underlying the various definitions of curriculum are perhaps more crucial than questions on the use of the word curriculum. Various value systems or ideologies have influenced the planning of various curricula. Perhaps three of the most important educational ideologies are classical humanism, progressivism, and reconstructionism.

Classical Humanism, perhaps the oldest ideology, concentrates on an elite minority. It held that "only small elite was to have the freedom to pursue enquiry and even for them only after a commitment to the value of the state has been inculcated." This ideology which is knowledge- centred certainly conflicts with attempts being made in the 20th century democratic societies to educate all young people.

Progressivism or child-centred education, also with a long history, represents a romantic rejection of traditional approaches to education. Instead of stressing the transmitting of a cultural heritage, what is more essential is "the need for the child to discover for himself and follow his own impulses." A curriculum with such a foundation "would be concerned not with subjects, but with experiences, topics selected by the pupils and 'discovery'" (Lawton 1983). Lawton rejects progressivism on the grounds that its view about human nature is visionary and it does not relate curriculum to knowledge or society.

The importance of social reconstructionism rests on the idea that education is a means of improving society. Skilbeck (1976) outlines reconstructionist ideology as follows:

1. the claim that education can be one of the major forces for the planned change in society
2. the principle that educational processes should be distinguished from other certain processes, such as political propaganda, commercial advertising, or mass entertainment, and that the former should, if necessary, enter into conflict with the latter in pursuit of worthwhile ends or goals;
3. the aspiration to make a new kind of person who would be better and more effective than the average citizen of today's society
4. an interest in core-curriculum in which prevailing social norms and practices are analysed, criticized, and reconstructed, according to rational democratic and communication values;
5. concept of learning and the acquisition of knowledge as active social processes, involving projects, problem solving strategies guided, but not dominated, by teachers;
6. the evaluation of teachers and other members of a carefully selected and highly trained elite of educators who are designated the agents of cultural renewal;
7. the relative neglect of difficulties and of countervailing forces- a characteristic feature of all kinds of Utopian thinking of which reconstructionism is "one of the recognizable strands".

The reconstructionist curriculum would emphasise social values, a stress which Lawton (1983) summarized as follows:

> "...in a democratic society, for example, citizenship and social coopration; knowledge is not ignored, but a 'why' question is never far away, and knowledge for its own sake is highly questionable; knowledge is justified in terms of individual social needs... For these reasons subjects will not be taken for granted to the same extent as in a classical humanist curriculum and various patterns of 'integrated studies' or faculty structures will tend to as sume more importance than subject departments..."

The ideas advanced in the following chapters shall be based mainly on a democratic kind of social reconstructionism. Although there may be value in the other two ideologies, the social reconstructionist ideology is seen to be most useful in a democracy because it allows for a more effective application of the principles of primary healthcare and community-oriented education for health professionals. Classical humanism and progressivism when compared with social reconstructionism are far less able to stand up to an analysis of the needs of individuals and communities. However, some components of their convictions can be used along or fused with social reconstructionism, as will be clear in the following chapters. The reconstructionists idea believes that education can be used not only to favor individuals but also to make society better.

Although the classical humanism and progressivism ideologies have influenced curriculum design, neither has adequately dealt with the significant impact of culture. In our 21st century it is imperative to recognize that curriculum development must be based on the culture of society and the student/teacher relationship.

Educational Focus on the Community

The basic principles and elements of primary health care (Chapter One) comprise an ideological framework that influences the education of health professionals. To place the concepts of PHC into education, the curriculum needs to be oriented to prepare, for example, nursing graduates:

> ...with the clinical and other skills necessary for them to serve as providers of primary health care; with the epidemiological knowledge to detect and prevent disease; with the understanding of behavioural responses required in order to promote healthful lifestyles; and with the organization and administrative ability to plan, manage and evalu

ate community health programmes. An inter-sector approach and involvement of the community are crucial and individual and communities should participate in decision-making on all health matters affecting them. The knowledge gained by nurses through professional training and experience must be shared with individuals, families and communities in order to generate local expertise and self- help... Students of [the health professions] need to be provided with a clear analysis of the structure and culture of the particular society they are educated to serve. (WHO 1986:.19)

The concepts of Primary Health Care that demand these changes in the education of healthcare professionals for the community are, as we have seen, the ideas that are integrated into the practice of community health care in homes, dispensaries, health centres and hospitals, which constitute the different levels of health care (WHO 1985), particularly in developing countries. Thus, the PHC concepts also provide the theoretical basis for the shifts in the educational focus to the community. Figure 2 (WHO 1985) presents the principal changes anticipated in the curriculum of a nursing school (the table is also applicable to curricula of other health professionals) when the emphasis changes from a conventional structure to community-oriented health care. Shifts to more community-focused education for health professionals due to the PHC concepts are already taking place in educational institutions for health professionals. Examples of the shifts are definitions of educational programmes designed to prepare health professionals for roles in the community. For instance, Schmidt et al (1991) define a community-oriented medical curriculum as a programme whose content considers the major health problems of a country where graduates of the programmes function. This means that firstly, the content of the programmes is not only based on the discipline that contributes to them, but also on the problems that characterize the programmes. Secondly, the particular character of the major health problems in a specific population differentiates one programme from another. Thirdly, because problems change from time to time, programmes are highly oriented to changes in the environment. Finally, the student activities in the programmes should include issues in health education and promotion, disease prevention, health research and involvement of people in improvement of their health status.

Figure 2: Comparison of Traditional and Community Health - Oriented Nursing Practice

Educational focus

Curriculum characteristics	Traditional nursing	Community-oriented nursing
Primary focus	Sick individual (pattern on curative model)	Community health (pattern on socioeconomic health model
Target population	Sick and disable seeking health care	Total population especially the underserved and high- risk
Primary setting for learning	Hospitals, other institutions, homes Communities,	homes, schools, industries, hospitals, and other institutions
Nursing role	Specialized and interdependent within the health sector	Generalized and interdependent within the health sector and health – related sectors
Nursing concerns	Conditions requiring hospitalization	Prevailing health problems and
Nursing practice	Primary care (nursing care of individuals) Patient/family participation in care Some follow-up of patients through hospital outpatient department	Primary health care approach Community/family/patient participation in care Identification and follow up of vulnerable groups. Health team approach
Problem–solving process: Assessment of problem-solving through individual and family	Individual and family needs and resources	Community/group/family/ individual needs and resources
Objectives of practice: Prevention – Therapeutic	Focus on secondary/ tertiary prevention Patient well enough to be discharged	Focus on primary prevention Improved patient, family, and community health, self-care
Health delivery system	Institutional and individualized care of patients	Primary health care for all; involvement of other sectors influencing health; health

Curriculum characteristics	Traditional nursing	Community-oriented nursing
Evaluation of nursing practice	Number of patients discharged from care by diagnostic category Frequency and intensity of patient contact	Percentage of coverage of population Service utilization rates by high-risk groups Rates of change in health status of high-risk groups/community Rates of response in treated groups, i.e., immunization, therapy complete coverage, average length of hospitalization, self –care ability and changes in health behavior

Source: WHO (1985)

Such an education must be a process that is transformative and developmental. Within an environmental plan, such education can take place at the various levels of an individual, organization, community and population. However, in all instances the learning is contingent on engagement and is socially constructed. Thus, the PHC concepts and principles also represent ideologies that contribute to the theoretical foundation for the change in the educational concentration from private or isolated healthcare settings to the community.

It has been suggested (e.g. Boaden et al 1999, Blair et al 2009) that there are sharp differences between developed and developing countries in the educational focus on the community that reflect the development of medicine and medical services in developed and developing countries. Information from WHO and from developing countries indicate that there are differences in opinion in terms of style and purpose of community practice and the education of professionals for such practice. These reflect the differences between the developed and developing world in terms of context and features of health systems and healthcare education.

Whereas developing countries have for many years focused on primary health care as a result of, among other things, dispersed populations, developed countries have relatively recently adopted primary care due to increasing high costs and demand for secondary and tertiary care (Boaden et al 1999). Also, whereas health care education has been subjected to professional control in developed countries, in developing countries health care education has been reformed because of the difficulties involved in adopting Western models of health care provision, such as high healthcare costs. As a result, developing countries integrated health care and professional education based on the PHC approach (Boaden et al 1999). In richer countries of the world that have also embraced the PHC approach, such integration of healthcare and professional education contingent on PHC has, as in developing countries, translated well in terms of innovations like association with key stakeholders with a shared vision, multidisciplinary working, peer-assisted learning, and widely disseminated teaching technology (Blair et al 2009).

However, despite the successes that many countries have registered through PHC implementation over the past 30 years, there are at least three main challenges (Schaay et al 2008) facing PHC that countries need to address:.(1) promotion of vertical programmes by development partners like the Global Fund that while providing much needed funding for priority diseases such as TB and AIDs have simultaneously promoted the selective approach of PHC through privileging vertically implemented and managed programmes (2) the influence of microeconomic forces resulting in weakening of healthcare systems due to fiscal austerity and the loss of the momentum around PHC and (3) health sector reforms that specifically concentrate on cost-effectiveness which limits the scope of PHC to a set of technical interventions and ignoring the determinants of ill health. In the constituents chapters of Part Two, we will look at how the potential opportunities and challenges of PHC and Community Health can affect planning a building a community of learning for community health in terms of the three strategic community processes of designing learning spaces, using information and communication technology, designing pedagogy, curricula and co-curricular activities for learning in the community.

Summary

This chapter has looked at the two contrasting interpretations of the term curriculum: curriculum as reality, curriculum as a prescription. The chapter has outlined perhaps three of the most important educational ideologies: classical humanism, progressivism, and reconstructionism. Also, the chapter has discussed the necessary changes in the curricula of health professionals who are required by the concepts of PHC and community health. In reviewing the definitions of curriculum and various educational ideologies, we have attempted to provide an understanding of the curriculum problem to provide perspectives from which to view the curriculum and the cultural analysis approach. Because education cannot be value-free, various ideological systems or values will produce various curricula. The premise of this book is the democratic kind of social recontruction-ism. The next chapter will consider various curriculum planning models which are based on this and other useful educational ideologies and through which such concepts of education can be given tangible forms as curriculum proposals in PHC/community health education.

3

Different Curriculum Planning Models

Curriculum models can be described as simplified ideas of reality in symbolic, mathematical or graphic form. Curriculum models help explain beliefs about the character of curriculum. There are many curriculum planning models in the literature that are used in health professional education. The models occur in two main categories, *prescriptive* and *descriptive* curriculum models, reflecting the two main approaches to defining the meaning of curriculum outlined above. They include:

(i)   the subject-centred model
(ii) the objectives model
(iii) the outcomes-based model
(iv) the process model,
(v)   the problem-based model and
(vi) the integrated model

Another model is the situational analysis model that is considered to be contemporary and well-constructed (Module 1: The curriculum in clinical Education 2005). Yet another model, Beattie's fourfold model (Beattie 1987), provides a useful example of how some curriculum models have incorporated both prescriptive and descriptive models in their structures, thus providing complex and multifaceted strategies to curriculum planners. These models are discussed in some detail in this chapter.

(i) The Subject-Centred Model

The Subject-Centred model (Module 1:The Curriculum in Clinical Education

2005) stresses the content of a course and allows teachers to indicate the subjects they wish to include in their courses. This prescriptive curriculum model is widely recognized as the principal feature of the traditional approach to planning education. Besides, it is the preferred approach for secondary schools and institutions of higher learning (Module 1:The Curriculum in Clinical Education 2005). In the same vein, it is a preferred approach for medical education (Module 1:The Curriculum in Clinical Education 2005)).

For medical education, where there is need to include subjects, its use is justified and necessary as it includes critical content such as epidemiology, infectious, diseases etc. On the other hand, it places emphasis on the essential values of studying a subject instead of its non-essential outcomes. It has therefore been overused, abused and abandoned for some kind of objectives model (Module 1:The Curriculum in Clinical Education 2005). Table 1 presents the advantages and disadvantages of the Subject-Centred model.

Table 1: Advantages and disadvantages of the Subject–Centred Model

Advantages	Disadvantages
• Students like it because it corresponds with their concept of what schooling is all about. Also they are used to it. • The step-by-step fashion by which skills are learnt suits traditional testing. Such learning can be easily quantified and explained to funding agencies, etc. • Quantifiable progress can be motivating to teachers and students • It is efficient in areas where resources for staff development are insufficient. • It is more accessible by teachers and students	• Prevents students from understanding the wider contexts of content • Concentrates on each subject in an individual context and does not allow students relationships between subjects • Discourages students from having a different point of view from what the teacher presents • Students are not part of the authority hierarchical upon which the approach rests

(ii) The Objectives Model

The objectives model (Tyler 1931) is perhaps the most well-known prescriptive curriculum model. It sets out what curriculum workers should do. It sets out to answer four fundamental questions which are based on Tyler (1931). The questions are:

- What educational purposes should the school seek to attain?
- What educational experiences are likely to attain this purpose?
- How can these educational experiences be organized effectively?
- How can it be determined that these purposes are being attained?

Figure 3: The Objectives Model

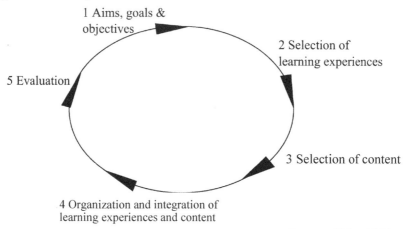

1 Aims, goals &
objectives

2 Selection of
learning experiences

5 Evaluation

3 Selection of content

4 Organization and integration of
learning experiences and content

Source: Tyler 1931

The model demands that curriculum planners must identify their objectives, plan the content and the methods by which the objectives are to be achieved, and finally try to measure the extent to which objectives are realized (Figure 3). This task must be done in a manner in which the four elements interact to influence and possibly change the design decisions for each other element. This model proposes that the beginning of curriculum planning must start with the objectives of the curriculum. This starts with specification of aims, which are often considered to be general statements of goals and purposes. Because aims have been regarded as too general and limited in specificity to serve as guidelines to curriculum planners, the process of curriculum planning has focused on formulation of more accurate statements of goals from the general aims which are usually called objectives. Table 2 shows advantages and disadvantages of the Objectives Model.

Table 2: Advantages and disadvantages of the Objectives Model

Advantages	Disadvantages
• It is useful in the area of training • It is appropriate in the provision of instructions	• It makes the induction of knowledge difficult • It places constraints on both the teachers and the pupils as it inhibits freedom of interaction that is central to the educational process • It demands the specification of objectives that are behavioural • It tries to be value-free like all scientific methods used in studying human action

	• It forces a hierarchical structure on curriculum planners and approaches education as an instrumental activity • Writing objectives is difficult and time-consuming, especially if as may be required each objective has to contain a statement of the 'behaviour' to be attained, the ' conditions' under which it would be demonstrated and the 'standards' by which it would be judged • It focuses on skills and knowledge acquisition only; higher order thinking skills, problem solving and values development are important educational functions that could not be written in behavioural terms.

(iii) The Outcomes - Based Model

The Outcomes - Based model (Module 1:The Curriculum in Clinical Education 2005) is a prescriptive model which proposes that curriculum should be defined by first thinking about the outcomes the planner wishes his or her students to obtain. The planner then works "backwards" to determine content, teaching and learning activities; assessment and evaluation. The use of Outcomes-Based Education (OBE) to underpin the curriculum process is becoming increasingly popular in health professional education (Davis 2003). OBE is often viewed as a return in another guise to the objectives model (Module 1:The Curriculum in Clinical Education 2005). Table 3 presents advantages and disadvantages of the Outcomes-based model.

Table 3: Advantages and disadvantages of the Outcomes-based Model

Advantages	Disadvantages
• Detailed descriptions of written outcomes give both teacher and student a clear picture of the competences to be attained at the end of the course • Teachers can adjust teaching methods to enhance attainment of stated objectives • Teachers can decide how objectives may be assessed. • Writing lists of competences or outcomes can be useful staff development lesson	• Objectives may unjustifiably be given greater role in educational processes • Teaching and learning processes may become so imposed and description and voluntariness are restrained • Constructing learning outcomes and competences can be difficult and time -consuming • Periodic re-appraisal of objectives and learning outcomes is an important requirement of course or curriculum development which is a continuous process

(iv) The Process Model

The Process model (Stenhouse 1975) is a descriptive curriculum model that emphasizes the use of principles to plan curricula and the educational process without the pre-specification of objectives. It focuses on the implementation of "worthwhile activities" that students can be involved in (Raths 1971) (Box 5). Such activities have their own built-in standards of excellence and can, therefore, be assessed. The premise of the model is that a form of knowledge has structure and it involves procedures, content and criteria. Content can be selected to exemplify the most important procedure, the key concepts, and the areas of situations in which the criteria hold.

It rests on the quality and judgment of the teacher rather than on the teacher's direction. Paradoxically, this point is also a disadvantage in that if the teacher is incompetent then the model cannot be successfully implemented. It is far more demanding on teachers and far more difficult to implement (Stenhouse 1975)

The model is committed to teacher's personal development as it offers a higher degree of professional development (Stenhouse 1975). Among other things, it takes account of the student's individual development and needs and motivates them to integrate new content into their teaching plans. Box 5 gives the list of Worthwhile Activities.

Box 5: List of Worthwhile Activities

- All other things being equal, one activity is more worthwhile than another if it permits students to make informed choices in carrying out the activity and to reflect on the consequences of their choices.

- All other things being equal, one activity is more worthwhile than another if it assigns students active roles in the learning situation rather than passive ones.

- All other things being equal, one activity is more worthwhile than another if it asks students to engage in inquiry into ideas, applications of intellectual processes, or current problems, either personal or social.

- All other things being equal, one activity is more worthwhile than another if it involves reality (for example, real objects, materials and artifacts).

- All other things being equal, one activity is more worthwhile than another if completion of the activity may be accomplished successfully by students at several different levels of ability.

- All other things being equal, one activity is more worthwhile than another if it asks students to examine topics or issues that citizens in our society do not normally examine – and that are typically ignored by the major communication media in the nation.

- All other things being equal, one activity is more worthwhile than another if it involves students and faculty members in 'risk' taking - not a risk of life or limb, but a risk of success or failure.
- All other things being equal, one activity is more worthwhile than another if it requires students to rewrite, rehearse, and polish their initial efforts.
- All other things being equal, one activity is more worthwhile than another if it involves students in the application and mastery of meaningful rules, standards, or disciplines.
- All other things being equal, one activity is more worthwhile than another if it gives students a chance to share the planning, the carrying out of an activity as planned, or share the results of an activity with others.
- All other things being equal, one activity is more worthwhile than another if it is relevant to the expressed purpose of the students.

Source: Raths (1971)

However, Goodson et al (1975) suggest that such a list of principles of procedure and worthwhile activities might result in a definition of activities before they begin, thereby imposing the interpretation of interactions. To prevent this, they suggest trying to produce a specification to which teachers can work, thus providing the background for a new procedure to plan curricula and the educational process. To achieve this, there is need to describe the type of encounter which best characterizes the new procedure through cooperative learning between teachers and students and among students. Chapter 10, which deals with pedagogical, curricular and co-curricular design presents a model of educational stages involved in learning clinical skills in the community (Boaden et al 1999) which includes a stage of cooperative learning.

As mentioned above, the idea of curriculum as praxis is in many ways a development of the process model, but unlike the process model it makes continuous reference to collective human well-being and the freedom of the human spirit. Among other things, it allows and encourages teachers and students to face the real problems of their existence and relationships, thereby confronting their own oppression (Infed 2010). Table 4 indicates advantages and disadvantages of the Process Model.

Table 4: Advantages and Disadvantages of the Process Model

Advantages	Disadvantages
- Gives much importance to active roles of teachers and learners - Gives much importance to certain activities because they are significant for life and in themselves - Projects lend themselves to the Process Model	- Overlooks consideration of appropriate content - Difficult to apply approach in some areas, such as areas where the emphasis is on development of practical skills - Does not lend itself so readily to measurement

(v) The Integrated Model

The Integrated model (Greeves 1984) is a descriptive curriculum model that allows planners to combine separate disciplines as a whole in the curriculum. The aim of integrating curriculum elements into a conceptually meaningful structure can be achieved through this curriculum model. Such integration can be at the level of the learner as well as the content or subject matter. The learner can be assisted by organizing the curriculum to analyze and apply the relationship of content, principles and concepts (Greeves 1984).

The use of the model overcomes the problem of instruction prescribed in the form of disparate subjects. Educational impact is further increased through the provision of relevant learning experiences at the same time. The approach helps to restructure knowledge to meet changing social needs. Students receive a wider, more in-depth comprehension of academic subjects and use what they learn to real-life situations, better preparing them to succeed in whatever endeavor they choose after school

By contrast, different subject areas may need different curriculum planning approaches, not an integrated approach. For example, a medical programme, where subjects are separate. It is also more demanding on curriculum planners and teachers in terms of time, energy and expertise (e.g, Stenhouse 1975). Table 5 presents advantages and disadvantages of the Integrated Model.

Table 5: Advantages and disadvantages of the Integrated Model

Advantages	Disadvantages
• Teachers have time to work together • Teachers deal with a limited number of students • Provides support to traditional curriculum • Offers scheduling flexibility to teaching teams	• Teachers can ignore the Integrated Curriculum • The work required to integrate subjects by teachers is time-consuming • As a result teachers are only able to implement an integrated curriculum for only a small portion of the school year

(vi) The Problem-Based Model

A problem-based curriculum (e.g. Loepp 1999 is another type of a descriptive curriculum model. It is identified by lessons in which students are presented with a specific practical, real, or hypothetical problem, or a set of problems, to solve. Problems are defined as having no stipulated correct solution, requiring knowledge construction on the part of the students, and demanding sustained attention beyond a single lesson. Problem-Based Learning (PBL) is a pedagogical approach and curriculum design methodology often used in higher education (Loepp 1999). Box 6 shows some of the defining features of PBL. Table 6 presents the advantages and disadvantages of the PBL model.

Box 6: Some defining features of PBL

- Learning is driven by challenging, open-ended problems with no one "right" answer
- Problems/cases are context-specific
- Students work as self-directed, active investigators and problem-solvers in small collaborative groups
- A major problem is identified and a solution is agreed upon and implemented
- Teachers adopt the role as facilitators of learning, guiding the learning process and promoting an environment of inquiry
- Rather than having a teacher provide facts and then testing students' ability to recall these facts through memorization, PBL tries to get students to apply knowledge to new situations. Students are faced with contextualized, ill-structured problems and are asked to investigate and discover meaningful solutions.

Source: Loepp (1999)

Table 6: Advantages and disadvantages of the PBL Model

Advantages	Disadvantages
<ul><li>It develops critical thinking and creative skills</li><li>It improves problem-solving skills</li><li>It increases motivation</li><li>It helps students learn to transfer knowledge to new situations</li></ul>	<ul><li>Students cannot really know what might be important for them to learn, especially in areas which they have no prior experience. Therefore teachers, as facilitators, must be careful to assess and account for the prior knowledge that students bring to the classroom.</li><li>A teacher adopting a PBL approach may not be able to cover as much material as a conventional lecture-based course.</li><li>It can be very challenging to implement, as it demands a lot of planning and hard work for the teacher.</li><li>It can be difficult at first for the teacher to become a facilitator, encouraging the students to ask the right questions rather than handing them solutions.</li></ul>

(vii) The Situational Analysis Model

Using this kind of descriptive curriculum model, the planner fully considers the situation or context in which the curriculum is located (Module 1:The Curriculum in Clinical Education 2005).,. Curriculum developers should ask about the significant internal and external issues (Reynolds et al 1976) that will impinge on the curriculum process. Box 7 indicates the external and internal factors of the situational analysis model:

Box 7: The external and internal factors of the Situational Analysis model

External factors

 Societal expectations and changes

Expectations of employers

Community assumptions and values

Nature of subject disciplines

Nature of support systems

Expected flow of resources

Internal factors

 Students

Teachers

Institutional ethos and structures

Existing resources

Problems and shortcomings in the existing curriculum

Source: Reynolds et al (1976)

This mode of analysis is among the five important stages in the curriculum process. They are: (i) Situational Analysis (ii) Goal formulation (iii) Programme building (iv)Interpretation and implementation (v) Monitoring, assessment, feedback and reconstruction. In using the Situational Analysis Model ((Module 1:The Curriculum in Clinical Education 2005).,. , no step should be left out and must be done systematically. But this does not mean that the steps have to be followed in a particular order.

This model is considered closer to an open-ended curriculum, because it requires the planner to consider the content of a curriculum and the external as well as the internal factors that impact on the context in which the curriculum is planned and implemented(Module 1:The Curriculum in Clinical Education 2005). Seen in this light, this model satisfies the important conception of the curriculum as a translation of educational ideas into practice. This and similar models, such as the Cultural Analysis model, and Beattie's Fourfold Model help us to define the essential elements of curriculum, namely situational analysis, statements of intent (aims, objectives, outcomes), content, implementation and organizational strategies, assessment, monitoring and evaluation.

However, this model might lock curriculum planners into another series of five steps which makes it difficult for them to tackle all the complexities curriculum work entails (Module 1:The Curriculum in Clinical Education 2005). Therefore, it has been suggested that though all these elements are inter-related, each essentially represents an important curriculum work open to its own investigation, debate and critique (Module 1: The Curriculum in Clinical Education 2005). But when they are taken together, they represent a comprehensive statement of the curriculum process. It must be borne in mind too that it is not easy to put all of them together and formulate simple principles for them. Table 7 presents the advantages and disadvantage of the Situational Analysis model.

Table 7: Advantages and disadvantage of the Situational Analysis Model

Advantages	Disadvantage
• The model is dynamic • Its elements are seen as interactive, undefiable and flexible • Its steps are conducted systematically but do not conform to a fixed starting point	• The feature that its steps are conducted systematically but do not conform to a fixed starting point can also be seen as a weakness.

(viii) Beattie's Fourfold Model

As indicated above, this model (Beattie 1987) incorporates both prescriptive and descriptive elements which are presented as four basic approaches for planning nursing curricula. These are:

- The curriculum as a map of key subjects
- The curriculum as a schedule of basic skills
- The curriculum as a portfolio of meaningful personal experiences
- The curriculum as an agenda of important cultural issues

Beattie's fourth approach is particularly interesting as it avoids providing detailed subject –matter, stressing instead contentious issues and political predicaments in healthcare. Issues such as power in healthcare are selected because they have no particular answer and are debatable, therewith encouraging inquiry and discussion. Furthermore, the model allows curriculum planners to use complex and multiple approaches. Table 8 shows the advantages and disadvantages of Beattie's Fourfold Model.

Table 8: Advantages and disadvantage of Beattie's Fourfold Model

Advantages	Disadvantage
• Integrates the theoretical and practical aspects, thereby bridging the gap between theory and practice • Gives a sense of balance for both teachers and students, as it integrates the four design elements with teaching methods, thereby providing for the various students' learning styles	When the four approaches are combined, the conventional approaches tend to dominate, resulting in the student centred ideas being included marginally.

Critique and Merits of the Curriculum Models

The objectives model (and similar prescriptive curriculum models we have looked at) is deemed insufficient for meeting these educational requirements of community health education because they are philosophically and psychologically not that practical and humanistic for such education. The model can only be used for particular kinds of low-level skills and not the entire community-oriented curriculum. The objective model is that of a close system, whereas in a democratic society individuals need to be autonomous through an open-ended curriculum, which is the hallmark of the descriptive curriculum models outlined above. However, such descriptive models that are more comprehensive and open-ended can be employed together with objectives (used in a restricted way) to provide a complex and multifaceted approach to curriculum planning that is much preferred to single model strategies.

An effort to solve the problem of objectives came as a proposal that each aspect of the curriculum should be examined separately on the premise that various curricula activities or subject areas will need different curriculum planning approaches. As a result of this, certain writers have proposed a different type of separation of curriculum activities that can be justified educationally from those that are instrumental, kinds of training for which statements of intent are not only acceptable but even necessary. This eclectic approach is a proper and acceptable approach to planning a curriculum for community health professional that fosters community of learning.

The advantages and disadvantages of the models outlined above, such as the subject-centred, objectives and process models can apply to Beattie's model as it includes the features of these models in its framework. However, there are two shortcomings of the models that have been suggested by Quinn (1995) that must be looked at. One shortcoming is that all the models, with the exception of Beattie's model, have all been formulated for the education of children; that the educational ideologies on which they are based are tenets of childhood education. Another imperfection suggested by Quinn is the failure of all the models, including Beattie's model, to consider the requirements and opinions of service managers/employers on the outputs they need from education and training to meet their service contracts. Some of these issues are addressed further in the following chapter on the Cultural Analysis Model.

Summary

This chapter firstly described several curriculum models that are useful for community-oriented education for health professionals. The objectives model and similar prescriptive models have been examined and considered inadequate, because they are impractical in relation to, among other things, the cultural values and behaviour and norms of a community. These models can only be applied to certain kinds of low-level skills and not the entire educational process, whereas in a democratic society individuals need to be autonomous through an open-ended curriculum. The following chapter describes a curriculum planning model on which this book is based, the Cultural Analysis Curriculum Planning model, which is open and has more to do with the descriptive nature of curriculum planning.

4

The Cultural Analysis Model

First, it is worth clarifying in this chapter the meaning of the terms culture and cultural analysis which are highly relevant if the cultural analysis approach is to be fully understood. Then, the chapter will describe the features of the ultural analysis model including its eight systems. Finally, the chapter will consider critique of the model, as well as its merits.

Definition of Cultural Analysis

Lawton (1983) who created the cultural analysis model defines culture as the total way of life of a society and the goal of education is to "make available to the next generation what we regard as the most important aspects of culture". Cultural analysis, according to Lawton, is the process by which a selection is made from the culture. The cultural analysis model when applied to curriculum planning would ask these questions:

(1) What kind of society already exists?
(2) In what ways is it developing?
(3) How do its members appear to want it to develop?
(4) What kind of values and principles will be involved in deciding on Question 3 and on the educational means of achieving Question 3?.

The cultural analysis approach (Figure 4) attempts to match the needs of individual youth within a specific society by carefully planning curricula. The election from the culture is made by analyzing the society that exists, how it got that way, where it is going, and then mapping out the kinds of knowledge and experience that are most appropriate. This process requires five kinds/

Francis Sarr

stages of classification:
(1) all the aspects that human societies have in common, such as social, economic, moral and other systems - the major parameters or cultural invariants, (2) the methods of analysis that can be used on a given society using the major parameters, or analyzing the differences between cultures in each of the systems-cultural variables, (3) classifying the educationally desirable knowledge and experiences- selection from culture, (4) consideration of the psychological theories and questions that are crucial for any curriculum development (this stage does not continue directly from the previous stages) and, (5) planning of the curriculum on the basis of the cultural analysis undertaken in the preceding stages taking into consideration the psychological theories and questions that operate on teaching and learning – curriculum organization.

Figure 4: Cultural Analysis Curriculum Planning Model

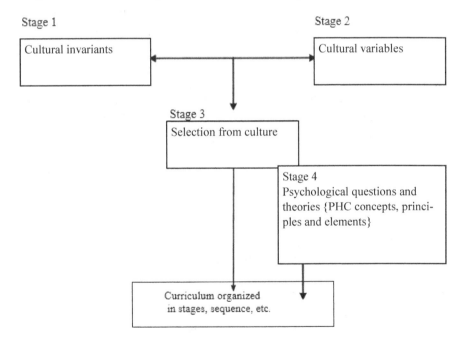

Adapted from Lawton, D (1983)

Cultural Invariants: Stage 1

Some Anthropologists have emphasized the differences between societies; others have stressed the similarities between all societies. Inspired by Lawton we shall look at the attributes that all humans seem to have in common, and then to examine how these can be related to education. As mentioned above, these human universals, Lawton calls cultural invariants. To describe cultural invariants, he creates and outlines eight headings. We present the eight categories with information from the relevant literature as follows:

- Social System
- Economic System
- Communication System
- Rationality System
- Technology System
- Morality System
- Belief System
- Aesthetic System

Social System

Every society must have some sort of social structure; even if there are only two people to interact there must be some definition of their relationships to each other and to their (albeit tiny) society as a whole. Kinship, status, role, duty, and obligation exist in every society and are passed from generation to generation. The social structure may be simple and taken for granted or complex and up for debate. It will be tied to economic, political and technical factors such as agriculture, health, tourism, foreign aid, or industrial production capacity. In the past, Western European societies were, for example, mostly rural and agrarian. The most important factor for the individual within that social structure was whether or not s/he owned land. As international trade and industry developed, however, land became less important than capital-the ownership of the means of production.

Economic System

Every society must have a means for dealing with the scarcity of resources, their distribution and exchange. Some economic systems may be as simple as barter while others may be impossibly complex, or anything in between. Marxist theory describes this as a continuum from primitive communism to feudalism to capitalism. There are a variety of methods available to analyze post-capitalist and capitalist economic systems. The amount of state ownership in basically capitalist systems, such as the USA, is an important measurable feature. Another important measure involves calculating the amount of the society's wealth that is controlled by the "top" 1% or 5% of the population. In addition, the structure of the government in power will have an inevitable effect on the economic system. For example: What kinds of skills and manpower are necessitated by the ruling political structure?

Francis Sarr

Communication System

Humanity, by its nature, communicates. The languages and methods may vary, but in every society of humanity there exists communication. Where the sole method of communication is oral, learning is informal-even unconscious as the child is unconscious of learning the language of its parents.

More usually, speech is not the only form of communication. Sign languages, various forms of signalling, pictography, or a codified writing system can accompany speech to form the communication system of the society. Most non-speech forms of communication are learned less automatically than speech, and must, to some degree, be taught. To the end of analyzing education, the rise of written language and printing is very important. This is because specialized learning becomes more available through printed materials and also encourages printed knowledge to become highly specialized and, so, less available to the lay member of the society. In democratized societies that claim open systems of education, one of the greatest problems is to achieve a balance between general education and specialization. This phenomenon is related to the media that are available to the general public and the specialized communication within a field of learning.

Rationality System

Every society is rational; that is, they have a system that defines what is reasonable. The different explanations may differ wildly, but attempts are always made to explain human behaviour and the phenomena of the universe as perceived by the society. A rationality system is fundamental to communication: words and signs must be based on rules of logic and meaning or mutual comprehension of society members, otherwise cooperation would be impossible. The rules of rationality can vary between societies however, whereas one society may claim that man is attracted to women due to love, another may claim the devil or witchcraft, while a third may invoke Sigmund Freud and his theory of the Oedipus Complex. Sigmund Freud's theory as related to the oedipal complex is basically saying that we humans are ruled "deep down" by animalistic sexual drives; that these drives are derived from our primitive ancestry and are hidden deep within our subconscious (Oedipus Complex Archives 1997).

Technology System

Man is characterized by his tools. Everywhere, we seek to dominate nature and not to be dominated by it. Early men devised tools to kill and butcher animals for food; they built shelters from the weather. Later, we developed agriculture and then complex machines. All humans are technologists in that they seek and use tools and attempt to pass on refinements and improvements to the next generation. Learning to use tools is always an important aspect of cultural life.

In some societies, due to the relative simplicity of their tools, inequities in access to the society's technologies are almost non-existent. In others the implements of the technology are so complex and diverse; no member of the society could possibly own or even learn to use all of them. Specialization and inequitable distribution of technology then become problems for the society to deal with. One problem in such societies is how to transmit all the skills to the next generation; another is the problem of allocation. Who learns what? Who accesses what? The different levels of learning that arrive thus will inevitably give rise to different levels of prestige or classes. This is the division of labour problem described by Durkheim (1993).

A society can be described by its dominant technology: is it simple or complex or in- between? Is the society pre-industrial or post-industrial? One could also catalogue, for example, the number of television sets or automobiles owned by the population of the society. But such measures are not useful. Broader categories are sufficient.

Morality System

All human possess a sense of the moral; all societies must, therefore, have a code of ethics that distinguishes right from wrong. What is considered right and wrong is by no means universal and can vary from society to society. It has been suggested that the moral feeling or conscience must be at least partly biological or genetic to account for their universality. Piaget (1965) and Kholberg (1989) have studied the development of moral ideas in children and their work tends to support this idea of a biological basis for moral feeling.

Some societies have a unified morality system that can be taken for granted, while others allow pluralism of ideas. In the latter type, socialization of children is more difficult because total agreement on the rules of behaviour to be transmitted does not exist. One way of categorizing morality systems is to ask the question: is the dominant morality religious or is it secular? Also consider whether the dominant morality is unified or if there are a variety of competing views as in most industrialized western societies.

Belief System

The belief system is closely connected to the morality system, but broader in scope. In some societies the moral code is backed up by and closely related to religious beliefs. In other societies the linkage between religion and ethics is weak or the ethical system is entirely secular and disengaged from the belief system. In this latter type of society the task of educating the young is made more difficult because children are taught to question and criticize rather than simply learn and accept.

In classifying belief systems, these terms may be useful: capitalist, socialist, democratic, totalitarian, liberal, conservative, etc.

Aesthetic System

People have aesthetic drives and needs. All societies produce some kind of art. This art has standards of form that can be related to the values of the society. There is an enormous variety of aesthetic forms, but nowhere are they absent from human life.

Approaches that categorize aesthetic systems relative to their evolution are not likely to be useful to us. For our purposes it is sufficient to define what counts as art in the society being examined. The boundaries between the arts and the relationships and categories we thus derive will be sufficient. Another useful area of study is aesthetic morality-the analysis of form and style in the arts.

Critique and Merits of the Cultural Analysis Model

As mentioned in Chapter 3, a reservation expressed by Quinn (1995) concerning the cultural analysis models (as well as other curriculum models) centers on the subject of childhood education. Quinn suggests that the cultural analysis model tries to use a rational system of analysis to the problem of curriculum content; that the model is meant for the curriculum of school children and addresses the work of curriculum planning in a general way. As evidence of this she cited Lawton's (1983) position on the topic: "the problems of young people growing up in a complex urban, industrialized society have been seriously underestimated; schools have generally failed to take seriously the moral, social and political aspects of culture in relation to curriculum planning"

When put another way this proposition, however, provides curriculum planners the means by which they can accommodate the realities in community healthcare we covered in Chapter 1, which were instrumental in the development of Primary Health Care, in the education and training of health professionals for the community using the cultural analysis approach:

> "the problems of health professionals functioning in the complex and increasingly changing community health systems have been seriously underestimated, community health training schools have often failed to take seriously the moral, social, political, economic and other aspects of culture in relation to curriculum planning".

The cultural analysis approach therefore has the distinct advantage that curriculum planners can address in their planning all the interrelated eight systems or characteristics that all societies have in common for the education of health care professionals for the community. Its use for such planning is based on the premise that it is impossible to train and educate adequately health professionals forthe community which is perplexing and constantly differentiating unless understanding of the eight features is included in their education and training. As mentioned earlier, lessons learnt through efforts at educating and training community health professionals (e.g., Schmidt et al 1991) and analyzing the causes of ill health (e.g. Peters et al 2009), for example, strongly suggest the need for the cultural analysis approach to such curriculum planning.

The cultural analysis framework can also be effectively used in planning community – oriented common curricula for health professionals, where the use of objectives can often prove to be problematic. As mentioned in Chapter three, the objectives model and similar prescriptive curriculum models have been looked at and deemed insufficient, because they are impractical in relation to, among other things, the cultural values and behaviour and norms of a community. The models can only be used for particular kinds of low-level skills and not the entire community-oriented curriculum. It is that of a close system, whereas in a democratic society individuals need tobe autonomous through an open-ended curriculum, which is the hallmark of the cultural analysis model. As Lawton says, "Cultural analysis is not an experimental science that can be described in terms of absolutes; it is an interpretive method in which we seek for meaning". Like descriptive curriculum models, such as the situational analysis model, the cultural analysis model views curriculum work as a complex human activity, it is grounded in the complexity of practice, and describes what actually happens in a conceptual way.

However, other descriptive models are deficient for planning a community-oriented curriculum for health professionals on their own because they do not cover all the eight elements of culture that allsocieties have in common. These eight elements, as already mentioned, are necessary for considering the realities of community health care as they help curriculum planners sufficiently take into accountthe economic, political, environmental, social, and other factors of culture which were instrumental in the development of Primary Health Care in the past three decades and will remain the major determinants of the health situation beyond the year 2000. However, the descriptive models, together with objectives (used only where necessary), can be employed alongside the more comprehensive and open-ended cultural analysis model that can consider all the necessary eight elements in the analysis. Thus, the cultural analysis framework provides a complex and multifaceted approach to curriculum planning that is much preferred to single model strategies.

The criticism that all the curriculum models outlined in Chapter 3, in addition to the cultural analysis model, fail to consider the requirements and opinions of service managers/employers on the outputs they need for education and training to meet their service contracts has been addressed by cultural analysis (Lawton 1983). When criteria of cultural analysis are applied to the issue of evaluation and accountability, cultural analysis methods would suggest that it is necessary to look at schools in a broader way and to establish goals on a wider scale than preparation for employment. It is important to look at the question of school efficiency not simply from one angle but from a variety of cultural viewpoints, using a complete cultural analysis approach. But, it is more useful to include external moderators, which may include managers/employers, in self-evaluation of schools than employing simple methods of evaluating the efficiency of schools on the basis of testing/examination. Accountability in schools, often seen as essential for efficient management, supervision and direction, tends to stress testing when applied to curriculum content. Therefore, in considering the relevance of models/systems of evaluation that are likely to appear in any national system of evaluation to cultural analysis, Lawton identifies the evaluation types that have more in common with cultural analysis: estimates of teacher competence, briefing decision-makers, teacher as researcher and case study.

Thus, while acknowledging the need to take into account the requirements of managers/employers concerning the results of education and training, cultural analysis views the business of meeting suchneeds as a democratic process, not an aspect of ministerial control. Clearly, this adds to the merits of the open-ended cultural analysis approach for planning a community – oriented common curriculum for the education and training of health professionals for the complex and increasingly changing community health systems. What is crucial is that health professionals are well educated and trained to deal with the realities of healthcare in the community.

Summary

This chapter has dwelt on the nature of the cultural analysis curriculum planning model. Any human group which does not possess all eight of the characteristics we have just discussed will not qualify as a society. The eight characteristics are derived from conventional definitions of society by the sciences of sociology and anthropology. They are more or less empirical in that no anthropologist has ever discovered a group of human beings living together permanently that lacks any of these characteristics.

All societies must not only have all eight of these systems, they must pass them to their offspring inorder to maintain a continuity of culture. Some societies achieve this through educational institutions and formal schooling. Where this type of education exists, it must contain certain features. For example, education must involve improvement as defined by the society. A satisfactory educational system must pass on the eight characteristics of the culture unless there are other agencies in existence to pass on some of them. As curriculum is defined as a selection from culture, we must ensure that the right selection is made from culture- all the eight systems described above.

From a health professional education perspective, cultural analysis is useful for planning community – oriented curricula for the education and training of health professionals for work in the complex and increasingly changing community health systems, where they must deal with the realities such as socio-economic and political factors that have affected healthcare in the past 23 years and will continue to do so in the future.

Having analyzed the eight systems as the most important cultural invariants that are usable in curriculum planning of health professional education and training for the community, we can now consider the application of the eight systems of cultural analysis to society.

5

Applying the Cultural Analysis Model

The application of the cultural analysis in this chapter involves viewing society generally in terms of the eight systems of culture already identified with particular reference to community health, and giving examples from Gambian society because it is the society that the author is most familiar with.

However, it is expected that curriculum planners would be wise to apply the cultural analysis model to the specific needs of their respective societies in order to be able to select from it what can be used to improve an existing curriculum or planning a new one. The study, therefore, progresses from a look at the critical similarities between all human societies, cultural invariants, to an examination of the dissimilarities of societies or cultural variables.

Cultural Variables: Stage 2

Social System

Countries can be classified according to their size, population, level of development, class, and the problems associated with these characteristics. For example, The Gambia, a narrow strip of land on the West Coast of Africa, is one of the smallest developing countries in the sub-region. Despite its small size, it is also one of the most densely populated countries in Africa. Like in many developing countries that are rural and agricultural societies, there is rapid urbanization which is mainly a result of disillusionment with the poor possibilities of agriculture and a hunt for employment which is hard to come by, migratory trends and factors attributable to historical developments, such as the expansion of the Mande Empire. This was a trading empire that spread in West Africa in the 13th–16th centuries. It grew from the state of Kangaba on the upper Niger River, founded probably before AD 1000. The Malinke inhabitants of Kangaba acted as middlemen in the gold trade in ancient Ghana. Growing in the 13th century under the leadership of Sundiata, it continued to expand in the 14th century and absorbed Gao and Timbuktu. It eventually outgrew its political and military strength, ceasing to be an important political entity by c. 1550 (The Free Dictionary 2010). The result of this is the spread of peri-urban shanty towns with overcrowding owed to over concentration of people in areas, inadequate housing, etc. This has put immense pressure on social, political, economic and educational structures, with the everlasting possibility for disease outbreaks as well as increasing problems of social control such as crime, which are characteristic of urban industrial societies. But developing countries may be unlike urban industrial societies like England where class not only entangles and increases the difficulties of such societies but also influences and at times have a hold over aspects of social life, such as education. For instance, The Gambia, like many developing countries, is a multiethnic country with different social and political features for each of its ethnic groups, but also with common social identicalness that intersects all ethnic lines. This is a result of a process of socialization that came from the people's mutual cooperation, and their many social experiences, like colonialism, introduction of western education and now the influence of the modern communication system. Because of all these, there is now a wide range of social organization norms and values that are common to all ethnic groups.

An important component of the social system in many developing countries is the household structure. This is characterized by large household sizes which mirror the prevailing extended family system. In the Gambia, for instance, there is the Kabilo System, a cluster of households that normally possess social and biological parameters, often with an elderly man as the head of the cluster. But perhaps the view of the cultural analysis approach and PHC, is a coping strategy for sustenance of livelihood which involves inter and intra-household transfer of resources.

Family organization in the Gambian traditional society, as in many traditional Africa societies, restson a peer-system which is at times inclined to favour one sex or the other. The function of these social units, which are grounded on age – sex cohorts, is mainly ceremonial and developmental. Though they may be good agents for development, their usefulness is limited by their sex-distinctness. Because of this, these social structures are imperfect for the purposes of bringing about needed development.

Another notable characteristic of the peer-groups in traditional African society is their age-grade, with the older-age peers acting for the younger age-peers in relation to ownership of assets (to a degree), management of assets and decision-making. In the Gambia, for example, the older-peer groups, especially, make up the Council of Elders, led by the Alkalo or Village Head. The Alkalo is responsible to the District Chief or Seyfo, who in turn is responsible to the Divisional Commissioner, the central government authority throughout the local government location.

The usefulness of this social and political framework inherited from the colonial powers is currently doubtful with regard to its sensitiveness for strengthening social partnership in favour of general social development. The disapproval aimed at such a structure concentrates on women's overall socio-economic involvement and women's empowerment in decision-making. Additionally, the framework is credited for the establishment and increase in the unjust dispensation of community resources, often on the basis of sex and age.

Also there are the peer-groups ceremonial functions. This particular feature of the peer-group comprises rites like circumcision, religious ceremonies, entry into adulthood, and so on. These practices are somewhat characteristic of certain areas of countries and specific to certain ethnic groups. Though traditions and customs are necessary for general social development, the expenditure on such events, instead of on more urgent requirements like education and health must be considered wasteful.

However, these widespread practices are not only important for economic reasons; they also have serious implications for health. One of such practices is early marriage, which is considered one of the main constraining factors for female education, employment and income, and further skills development. Other related health and social problems include poverty, resulting from large families, and high infant and maternal, morbidity and mortality. Cowley (1991) notes that such health patterns have many consequences: "societies may [among other things] deal with the frequent death of their children by placing a high cultural value on large families, forming only loose emotional attachment to children and showing great veneration for the elderly". Polygamy and similar social practices are as costly as they are complicated. The practice of sexual relationships with multiple partners in and out of wedlock results in the prevalence of sexually transmitted diseases and other related health problems like spontaneous abortion. Such problems are magnified by rapid urbanization and mobilization.

Another widely experienced social practice that has much relevance for health is Female Genital Mutilation (FGM). Female Genital Mutilation is a general term for a variety of surgical operations carried out on girls and women primarily in twenty-eight African countries and among some minorities in Asia. It is the partial or total removal of the female external genitalia including the clitoris, labia, mons tissue over the pubic bone, and the urethral and vagina openings. Despite the growing opposition to this practice, mainly because of its social and health consequences, it is still extensive. The reason for this rests, to a large extent, on the contentions surrounding the issue, some of which are misunderstandings with religious basis. There is a conflict between international human rights and the doctrine of cultural sovereignty which is ongoing and controversial. Critics of international human rights law argue that the international community uses treaties to limit national tradition in the health system. Such pluralism provides a wider range of choices on medical treatment and therefore makes health seeking behaviour hard to understand. Also, as we shall see later, the various health systems influence each other and there is often a hierarchical order that rests on prestige and power between the different medical traditions. This situation often results in more powerful traditions (e.g. medical doctors) exploiting or suppressing feeble traditions (e.g. traditional healers).

We have also seen that there are various levels of organization within Gambians health system. This concept of different levels is helpful in understanding the distribution of political power and economic-resources for the improvement of health. In addition, as shall be clear in the following sections, these important factors of health development are equally apportioned between the different levels of the health system.

Hardon also arranges the various medical practices and ideas in a society by differentiating various incompletely agreeing health care sectors. For instance there is the popular sector, including the new professional lay- persons who initially identify and treat illnesses by different traditions in healthcare. Another is the folk sector, made up of traditional healers like herbalists, etc. Finally there is the professional sector, the group given privileged status with personnel such as medical specialists, who practice through conventionally acknowledged professional standings, etc.

As can be seen from the above discussion, this differentiation is identifiable in the Gambian health system (as well as the health systems of other developing countries). But perhaps the greatest value of this framework from the point of view of the cultural analysis model is the stress it makes on, among other things, mental processes such as beliefs systems on health and illness which are different, and sometimes even conflicting. As shall be clear in the following sections such cognitive processes are on beliefs about the causes of illness and appropriate therapy.

Economic System
Developing countries in general can be classified as agricultural societies that

are striving to develop industrial sectors. This is because, among other things, employment and incomes are highest in the industrial sectors compared to the agricultural sectors. For instance, the main feature of the Gambia's economy is its heavy dependence on agriculture and on a small number of cash crops, mainly groundnuts, its narrow economic base and its small size. The dominance of agriculture is underscored by the value of activities undertaken in this sector. Over half of the arable land is under groundnut cultivation, and also, an equal number of the population is engaged in groundnut cultivation, in addition to livestock raising and subsistence farming. This predominance is mainly due to its vulnerability to the climatic conditions and to the shifts in international markets for agricultural products.

The industrial sector in the Gambia, for example, is very small indeed. It includes manufacturing activities confined to light industries like groundnuts, milling, and provides employment for only a small number of the labour force. Also, it includes fisheries which, though an important foreign exchange earner, are threatened by coastal erosion, especially the first landing sites along the coast.

Another important component of the industrial sector, which is an important source of income for the country, as for many other developing countries, is tourism. This, however, provides employment for a small number of people. Also, there are commercial activities which rely heavily on re-export trade to neighbouring Senegal and other countries within the sub-region of West Africa, and are vulnerable to the economic policies of these countries.

The economies and financial situations of many developing countries faced a period of decline progressively from the middle 1970s due mainly to improper micro-economic policies and opposing exogenous factors. This prompted the governments in these countries by mid-1980 to embark on essential modifications in economic policy. In the Gambia, as in many Africa countries, such changes came in the form of structural adjustment programmes aimed at improving and sustaining economic performance.

While the Gambia, for example, registered some micro-economic achievements from these measures, such as stabilizing the economy and producing a steady significant growth, the country's social indicators still ranked low: Low standard of living, life expectancy and literacy, and high infant and maternal mortality, poverty, and unemployment (Ministry of Health & SW 1998).

It is evident that in periods of economic decline social and educational contradictions are inclined to become more evident, perhaps increasing the divide between the rich and the poor in relation to what is provided for education and welfare. In fact the consequences of Gambia's Economic Recovery Programme, for instance, were mostly felt by the poor. Also, the health and education sectors were more vulnerable to this situation which is likely to remain in the future.

Indeed, in recent years, the financing of the public health sector which comes from three sources:
government (through allocation for general revenue funds in recurrent and development budgets), donors (through contributions in development budget and other external assistance), and communities (through cost-recovery systems) has been decreasing substantially.

Though the health sector has the second largest budget after education, recent expenditure patterns show a great decrease in the total allocation of overall government expenditure to the health sector. The same pattern also applies in terms of recurrent expenditure and health expenditure as percentage of GDP, which continues to be an extremely low proportion of the domestic resources directed to health care by government (Ministry of Health & SW 1998).

Despite the financial constraints, priority is being given to secondary levels of care (health centres and dispensaries) in the allocation of the limited resources. Specialized programmes which cross the whole health system, such as community health and family health, also benefit from the re-direction of resources from urban to rural health care. However, the improvement and sustainability of the gains in financing health services and equitable distribution of scarce resources will remain a challenge (Ministry of Health & SW 1998).

Communication System

The key form of communication in most societies, if not all, is human language. In many countries most people speak a native language, such as Mandinka in West Africa, but there may be also minority languages that are spoken as first or second languages. Thus, the language structure in many countries is multilingual. Each of the many ethnic groups in the Gambia, for example, has its own language, but because of a process of culturalization – migration, trade, inter-marriages, conquest, etc., people's language cross ethnic groups. However, some languages are most widely spoken than others, which is much a reflection of the demographic profile (large population) of the ethnic groups who have these languages rather than their failure to respect the language customs of other ethnic groups. Because of mutual co-existence and common social experiences, as mentioned earlier, The Gambia also enjoys strong commonalities of language systems.

In many developing countries like the Gambia the language structure includes English as the official language, which is a legacy of colonialism. However, the popularity of English in these countries is not only due to colonization. English is now a far more universal language than Latin was in its heyday. Apart from being the language of international airline pilots, English is also a common tool of commerce, entertainment, stage craft, scholarship and the dominant language on the Internet. It has been estimated by British experts that by the year 2000, more than one billion people on the planet, and roughly one out of six people will be speaking or studying English. (Newsweek 1997) Indeed, not only has it been suggested that the English language is now the operating standard for global communication, research has shown that for scientific subjects the proportion of all material on the Internet in English is around 70-80% (The Economist 1996). Communication System The key form of communication in most societies, if not all, is human language. In many countries most people speak a native language, such as Mandinka in West Africa, but there may be also minority languages that are spoken as first or second languages. Thus, the language structure in many countries is multilingual. Each of the many ethnic groups in the Gambia, for example, has its own language, but because of a process of culturalization – migration, trade, intermarriages, conquest, etc., people's language cross ethnic groups. However, some languages are most widely spoken than others, which is much a reflection of the demographic profile (large population) of the ethnic groups who have these languages rather than their failure to respect the language customs of other ethnic groups. Because of mutual co-existence and common social experiences, as mentioned earlier, The Gambia also enjoys strong commonalities of language systems. In many developing countries like the Gambia the language structure includes English as the official language, which is a legacy of colonialism. However, the popularity of English in these countries is not only due to colonization. English is now a far more universal language than Latin was in its heyday. Apart from being the language of international airline pilots, English is also a common tool of commerce, entertainment, stage craft, scholarship and the dominant language on the Internet. It has been estimated by British experts that by the year 2000, more than one billion people on the planet, and roughly one out of six people will be speaking or studying English. (Newsweek 1997) Indeed, not only has it been suggested that the English language is now the operating standard for global communication, research has shown that for scientific subjects the proportion of all material on the Internet in English is around 70-80% (The Economist 1996).

Despite English being the official language in many developing countries and despite its global importance, it is seemingly not given the attention it deserves. The English language problem in these countries is acute not only in schools, but also in streets and, surprisingly enough, in media houses, as is evident from listening to numerous public addresses by public officials to know that the English problem is common.

Other important forms of communication require consideration for the purpose of planning education for PHC and community health. The use of mathematics is emphasized in the democratic societies that are struggling to become more scientific, industrialized and developed. The need to learn computer language, and the understanding and use of signs and symbols to help one survive and be successful in such societies must be stressed. Technical jargon and other kinds of language resulting from division of labour created by industrialization, coupled with the development of printing, which cannot be understood by non-health professionals like policy makers also, require consideration. Also, the mass media in developing countries is becoming an important characteristic of the communication system. For example, the Gambia now has a TV station, in addition to several FM radio stations in and around the capital, and many rural broadcasting stations, but as reports (e.g., UNICEF 1998) reveal, the majority of Gambians cannot afford TV and radio sets and thus access to health information from these sources is limited. The problem is compounded by the clearly visible lack of ownership and control of broadcasting and broadcasting programmes in rural areas; the delivery of programmes is not approached in a participatory manner that can involve farmers and rural people in the planning and broadcasting of rural radio programmes. So far, radio broadcasting to rural communities focuses mainly on delivering instructional sensitization materials.

Rationality System

The Protestant Reformation in English in the 16th and 17th centuries marks the beginning of the country's rationality system. This historic event questioned authority and resulted in a "rational" interpretation of the universe. Several other scientific efforts also contributed to the development of the English rationality system which interprets change and considers change as realistic. Thus England, like other industrialized countries, can content with quick social and technological change. Thus, in England and other industralised countries the kind of knowledge which seems to be most important is the scientific form. While many developing societies with high illiteracy rates, among other things, may not fall under the category of countries where science is predominant, the efforts at modernization, and the social and technological changes that go with such developments are necessarily giving science a higher role. However, the high status of science has not only misinterpreted the disciplines involved in the study of human behaviour, it has also concealed the requirement to understand other ways of thinking and assessing what might be used in the aesthetic and other experiences. As will be clear in the following paragraphs, this has much meaning for a PHC/ community health and cultural analysis-type curriculum for health professional education, where, like all kinds of education, 'utilitarian, thinking has a tendency to be most important.

Technological System

The kind of technology system by which people in both developed and developing countries try to control the environment consists of simple and complex technologies, and between these two kinds of technologies. The majority of people living in the rural areas of developing countries, for instance, engage mostly in agriculture where simple tools are used. In mainly the urban and peri -urban areas, however, technology is more complex. There are specialization and division of labour which are involved in the economic and political systems of the countries.

There has been widespread acceptance of "appropriate technology" in recent years, which in industrialized societies means "technologies that are ecologically well adapted to the local environment, small in scale, and sparing of such natural resources as energy" (Jequier 1981). Two examples to illustrate this: President Clinton in an address to the Delaware General Assembly during his presidency mentioned the use of technology without damage to the environment as one of the important challenges that the U.S government must face now and in the future. The 1998 G8 Summit held in Birmingham, England, ended with economic and environmental issues, such as greenhouse emissions, forests and deforestation.

In developing countries the term "appropriate technology" refers to "a wide range of low-cost technologies aimed specifically at meeting the most basic needs of the world's poorest people", with particular focus on health, nutrition, food production, employment and housing (Jequier 1981). Many developing countries are now striving to meet the goals of such appropriate technology. For example, in September 1998, a Permanent Inter-state Committee for the Control of Drought in the Sahel (CILLS) regional conference, with the theme: "Environment Friendly Integrated Pest Management.", was held in Banjul, The Gambia, to discuss related technological, environmental and agricultural issues. There are also more practical examples. For instance, an American professor of agriculture once told students of an African university about what he said was a unique experience in the area of agronomy: a local farmer showed him how a simple method is used by farmers to determine or identity the quality of soil –through mere observation of the nature of soil on anthills. Health professionals must appreciate such appropriate technologies and develop interest in searching for ways they can be further developed and used in, for example, improving the supply of food and, consequently, the nutritional status of rural communities.

The growth of "appropriate technology" in health care has been accompanied by increasing efforts to assess their potential dangers and to compare them with their possible values. The need to base policy decision on evaluations on health technologies is being realized in the field of health, where the main interests are issues such as safety, cost and efficacy of health technologies. The connection between the education of health professionals for PHC/community health and health technologies is therefore a very crucial issue to discuss, and this will be done in the following chapter.

Morality System

Because countries are generally multiethnic societies, they are also morally pluralistic societies. Moral thinking is grounded mainly on the different religious, societal norms, practices, traditions, and values that exist for different ethnic groups. Though a secular state, the majority of the population in the Gambia, for example, are Muslims with Christianity and other religions denominations numbering only a small portion of the population. Consequently, one can speculate that, generally, traditional norms and values as well as moral thinking are based mainly on religious principles.

However, the influence of Islamic and other religious principles vary according to where a person lives. In the urban areas of the Gambia where more than one third of the population who are mostly Muslims live, traditional norms and values systems that influence people's lives in the rural area are being replaced by decisions directed by informed choices and actions governed by the common- law, that is based on the British Common-law, and has changed over the years (Goodwin 1998). Factors contributing to such change include high percentage of informed people, modernization and higher literacy rates.

The common- law and equity, and the customary practices and Sharia (Muslim) laws make up the legal system. The exercise of judicial powers is through the superior courts, such as the supreme courts, cadi courts and lower courts like district tribunals. The cadi courts have jurisdiction in marriage, divorce and inheritance matters in the Gambia. Decisions of these courts are appealed at the Cadi Appeals Panel. The courts preside over matters affecting Muslims and any other persons who opt to go to these courts.

In exercising their powers, the courts and other organs or groups concerned should be non-partisan. They can only be imposed upon by the constitution, which is the supreme law of the country. The powers of religious laws, especially the Sharia which represents the personal law of the Muslims, have social and health implications for Gambians, particularly for Gambian women and children. These laws are biased in favour of men as shown by, for example, the practice of unequal distribution of property after death between male and female siblings (Goodwin 1998).

It seems that developing countries are beginning to experience the difficulties that are complicating the moral scene in developed societies. One of these is immigration from non-Muslim and non-Christian societies. Another is the view that law and morality, which have a strong connection in Gambian society, for instance, should be separate. In the Gambian context, this has particular relevance in terms of gender issues and cultural practices that affect people's welfare and health. For there is the tendency for people not to know what the rules of societies really are. Also, there is the hint that morality is simply a matter of taste; that no rule is better than another.

The importance of the persistent real differences of moral/cultural values has been shown by, for example, a poll (Newsweek 1996) in which 50% of respondents say adultery is wrong because it is immoral; 25% because it can break up a marriage; 17% because of the danger of AIDS and other diseases". Ignatieff (1998) suggests that demands for moral intervention should not conceal such differences in such values. He writes:

"...If the essential facts about the human situation is that our values conflict- that cultures and societies place significant different accents on the rights of individuals vis-a- vis the collectivity- then moral intervention has no choice but to become a highly complex experience of inter-cultural translation, in which each side tries to negotiate its way to a shared understanding which may change each other's values but does not violate each other's moral identities...."

As will be clear in the following chapters, this suggestion has much relevance for planning the education of health care professionals using the open cultural analysis curriculum planning framework.

Belief System

Because of the close interconnectedness between the morality and belief systems, the difficulties in a country's morality system are characteristic of the problems of the belief system regarding the seemingly absent consensus and the increasing dangers in the moral scene in developed countries outlined above, which developing countries are now also experiencing.

Again, one can say that this situation is gradually growing in the belief systems of developing countries, particularly in the urban areas, due to factors mentioned earlier: modernization, education, communication, etc. However, like the morality system, beliefs in developing societies in general, vary according to ethnicity, tradition, religion, and societal norms and values. For example, in the Gambia, Islam, as in the morality system, exerts the strongest influence because of the holy wars, trade, and the fact that Islam had been able to accommodate societal values and practices that were rejected by Christianity (Goodwin 1998).

At the other end of the culture spectrum are still those few who have rejected Islam and Christianity altogether. These people worship idols, dead ancestors and spirits, but ultimately believe in the one supreme God. Those "in-betweens", who belong to certain ethnic groups, are not completely converted to either Islam or Christianity, as is evident in their behaviour in times of trouble with those ethnic groups (Goodwin 1998) This situation is reflected by belief systems about health care. Some beliefs which are of health importance seem to cross ethnicity, religion, tradition, etc, while others are specific to the different social groups. For example, reports on State Registered Nurses' community field experiences in a rural area of The Gambia, show that beliefs on the causes of disabilities are attributed to several factors in this order of importance: God (meaning that it is God's will and therefore nothing can be done about disabilities); illness; witchcraft; marabous (evil spell); evil forces (evil spirits); old age.

The following show other characteristics of the belief systems in developing countries:

"...women with twins are always advised with superstitious beliefs and ta-boos about twins. They are told that whenever one of the twins gets sick, the only cure is for the mother to beg or else no doctor could remedy the situation. In fact in some instances they have created a taboo that if any of them is given something while the other is deprived, that leads to the suffering and sickness of parents..." (Daily Observer 1997).

"...Africa is full of evil: witchcraft, juju-juju, black magic, taboos that have their roots in questionable customs and traditions. Satanism, you name it, it is practised somewhere in Africa. The effects of so much evil permeate our socie-ties in the form of political conflicts, religious dissensions, family strife's... Today, evil is more apparent than good and many live in fear of the repercus-sions of coming up against evil..." (Daily Observer 1998).

Aesthetic System

Like the technology system, a country's aesthetic system consists of tradi-tional as well as modern forms of art and entertainment. Some arts and enter-tainment may be associated with the majority of people living in a country at the subsistence level, such as painting of clothes and drama. Others forms, such as architecture, may be linked to upper classes, who are usually found in the urban and peri-urban areas of a country.

However, as we mentioned above, different value systems exist for different ethnic groups in many countries, although strong commonalties for some value systems across ethnic groups exist. Furthermore, many countries are secular states which are becoming increasingly pluralistic due to factors such as urbanization, modernization, migration, the influence of modern communication system, etc. Therefore, in such societies it is difficult to define what art is, even the criteria for deciding what is good art or bad art are inconclusive and may be questioned openly in public.

There are problems of the aesthetic system that are linked to difficulties and contradictions inside the social fabric. There is often the belief in many industralised countries that divergent criteria apply or simpler every day happenings do not deserve much aesthetic attention. This separation between art linked to upper classes and other aesthetic experiences which deserve to be considered as art but are treated differently is considered unjustified (Lawton 1983). However, in developing countries where the class system is perhaps comparatively less visible and where many people share values in common these difficulties and contradictions, if they exist at all, seem to be less important in the lives of people. While this may be so, in the context of cultural analysis and the proposed common curriculum, however, it is more important to consider the importance of the kind of aesthetic experiences such as art and entertainment like pictures and drama that can be used in health care (Butt et al 1997). Aesthetic experiences that can communicate important health messages on nutrition, etc, whatever criteria is attached to them, and whether or not such experiences belong to one class or another. This will be discussed in more detail in the following chapter.

To further demonstrate the applicability of the cultural analysis framework to community health let us take as an example the issue of discrimination against disabled persons in society. In Nepal (Schoberg 2010), for instance, where today both Hindu and Buddhist beliefs intermingle, religion holds that the deeds of past lifetimes, whether good or bad, determine future lives. However, in the rural areas where long-dated rituals are performed and access to health care is inadequate, people believe that disabilities are a permanent fate. The result of this fatalistic judgment is that parents force their disabled children to beg in the streets or hide them at home. The psychological fallout of such discrimination is that disabled persons feel that they don't deserve an opportunity, among other things. This socio-cultural problem in this community is clearly based on religion which, as the analysis of the social, morality and belief systems shows, has a strong influence on peoples' lives. The perception that disabilities are a fixed end is especially a characteristic of the belief system. The problem of limited access to modern health care in this developing country that seemingly results in people maintaining or reverting to traditional medical practices has been suggested by the analysis of especially the social and economic systems.

Doing something about this problem rests on the view that it is unjust to discriminate against disabled persons. Such moral thinking, as we have seen in the analysis of the morality system, is grounded mainly on the different religious, societal norms, practices, traditions, and values that exist for different ethnic groups. The actual measures that can be employed to change this perception in society show how community resources that can be identified in analyzing the social and economic systems are used. Such resources include notable, popular or useful persons in the community like film stars, journalists, athletes, etc, that can participate in marketing campaigns and other public education strategies aimed at changing the perception. Analysis of the economic system can also indicate the needed local and international sources of funding, such as grants from a local Rotary club or WHO office. The important roles of the communication, technology and aesthetic systems are demonstrated in terms of the ways communication technologies and strategies can be used in the campaign to change the mindset of society, such as a film star appearing in television and radio ads that can be broadcast across the country, street theatre, comic strips and newspapers. And research can be employed before and after a campaign to measure attitudes towards people with disabilities, which clearly demonstrates how analysis of the rationality system can be useful in initiating and enhancing community health initiatives.

This account shows not only how each of the eight systems of the cultural analysis framework are applicable in community health, but also the interrelatedness of the systems. For instance, the argument that religion and abortion are mutually exclusive is fallacious. The reason why abortion is so controversial is because such public health/community health issues are also religious issues, as cultural analysis clearly demonstrates. Using the cultural analysis approach to curriculum planning, community health professionals can be prepared to deal with such social, political, economic and other challenges in community health care.

Summary

In summary, this chapter has clearly shown that there are many constraints and challenges that are linked to both developed and developing societies. These produce discord that may lead to separation particularly in societies where belief systems and moral prescriptions are unclear. The cultural analysis in this chapter seemingly suggests deterioration in many of the systems of both developed and developing societies, more so in some systems than in others.

For example, clearly developing countries have to deal more with economic decline than developed countries. On the other hand, it seems that industrialized societies are facing greater difficulties in their belief andmoral systems when compared to developing countries where belief and moral thinking systems are relatively more identifiable. The function of the cultural analysis framework is to provide curriculum planners a framework as a means of planning the education of health professionals who must deal with these difficulties and challenges in the community health systems they operate. The following chapter looks at the selection from the eight systems of culture for coverage in the common curriculum for health professional training and education for the community.

6

A Selection from the Culture

This chapter shall now consider the selection from the eight systems of culture by looking at the degree to which the eight systems should be covered by present subjects, and suggest the quality and appropriateness of such coverage in health professional education for the community. Like the application of the cultural analysis framework, this selection will be done generally in terms of the eight systems of culture already identified. It will also give examples from Gambian society because it is the society that the author is most familiar with. However, it is also expected that curriculum planners would be wise to select from their specific societies what can be used to improve an existing curriculum or planning a new one.

Social System

Countries generally have various complex systems of values and beliefs, social organizations and practices, although there may be differences from one country to another. Notwithstanding, health professionals often lack an in-depth understanding of the wide scope of social factors including political factors that affect people' health. The consequence of this has been an inclination to provide clinical care without regard for the circumstances of people's lives. Such a limitation makes the application of the PHC/community health concepts and principles, such as prevention impossible.

As we noted in the previous chapter, there is now often a tendency to give science greater emphasis, with the belief that objectivity is more important than other sorts of criteria. Clearly, the only way to fill such a gap is to emphasize in the common curriculum acknowledgement of the significance of personal values and beliefs in health care etc. Also, an enriched understanding of the importance of socio-cultural factors in disease prevention, and the presentation, diagnosis, consequences and management of illness, is crucial. Accordingly, a significant amount of the teaching must be allocated to relevant applied psychosocial science, including political science. For such teaching to be effective, it must be integrated with the systems in which the health professionals function. This will provide the health professional opportunities to use his newly acquired knowledge, skills and techniques and can be convinced of the need not to return to old practices. One of the former practices that health professionals giving care and community groups who should be involved in health care must not revert to, and which the common curriculum must address, as the analysis suggests, is to work alone instead of collaborating with others in a team. Health workers often consider working alone quicker and more relaxing than working in a team, where they are likely to face problems of discord. But it is clear that working alone does not allow for the causes of ill health to be adequately dealt with. The way to fill this gap is to ensure that the common curriculum provides opportunities for sufficient development of the health professionals' skills of negotiation, mediation and advocacy so that they can collaborate effectively with people in and outside the health sector. In this regard, students must also be helped to see all people as equal, disregarding feelings of superiority to recipients of care and inferiority to higher authority.

There is another contradiction in the social system suggested by the analysis that the common curriculum must cover. This is the reward system which in Western traditional clinical care is based on the cure of disease, or decrease in suffering as a consequence of the knowledge and skills of health professionals. Health professionals are rewarded for such achievements by the gratitude of their clients, etc. However in primary health care/community health care settings such rewards are less visible. To fill this gap, the common curriculum must include opportunities for helping students to develop understanding of and skills in affecting changes in the reward system in accordance with changing circumstances. Such changes include changes in both intrinsic rewards, such as income and status that can motivate, and extrinsic rewards like personal satisfaction.

There is another implication for the common curriculum that is also reflected by the analysis. This relates to the roles and status of community groups such as women and children. As has been mentioned, although more rural people are now making decisions based on informed choices and action, there are misunderstandings of religious guidelines on issues such as gender issues. One can say that, generally, traditional values and norms for women and children are grounded on such principles. This calls for not only adequate understanding of roles and status of women and children in traditional society, but also the inter-working of these conventional rules in relation to the wide guidelines of conventions on the rights of women and children especially. Associated with such difficult matters is gender empowerment in regard to critical social issues, which include arrangements for traditional marriage, ownership, the right to education and work, particularly for the girl child, inheritance and female genital mutilation. For example, in many developing countries there are contradictions between how the female is seen in the informal place and the formal workplace, such as assignments to activities that are unfair and stereotypical and undermines the female chances to get access to good jobs for the assumption is that they will not do well.

Certainly, all these will require sufficient coverage in the common curriculum of understanding of relevant legal and ethnic considerations and policy processes, including legislative processes. Such content should provide opportunities for studying the actors within the policy process, the external forces influencing it, and the mechanisms within the political system for participation in related policy making. Learning in these critical areas must bear upon state-centered as well as society-centered approaches that are set within a global context. In addition to such content, the common curriculum must provide opportunities for developing skills for sensitization to the issues, particularly health education of rural communities. For instance, lack of communication (and education) is a main factor that allows the spread of female genital mutilation which the curriculum should address. Success in legislation on the practice of female genital mutilation in Africa, where it is common but where there is often no age of consent in the legal code, has been difficult to achieve. This is because laws were enforced without initially generating sufficient social awareness on the issue. This has caused resistance to change.

Accordingly, the student must be grounded in the planning, implementation and evaluation of relevant health education and communication approaches, especially approaches that are suitable for rural communities. Such health education must emphasize prevention of serious health problems like vaginal infection, the health consequences of harmful social and cultural practices, health counselling, etc.

Economic System

The Primary Health Care Strategy adopted in especially developing countries should be implemented cost-effectively. But health professional often lack the required knowledge of resources utilized for primary health care and of the results obtained. There are two main areas (Carrin et al 1992) that should be addressed in the common curriculum. The first concerns the necessity of health professionals' understanding of economic approaches to the analysis of the health sector in order to understand its connection to the total economy. The second area deals with the need for efficient and equitable use of resources, especially in view of the severe financial constraints in especially developing countries.

The first area of learning that the common curriculum should address, therefore, includes understanding of macro-economic analysis which can cover major issues raised by the analysis of the national economy. One issue is whether the health sector is given a fair portion of government budget reductions. The other issue is the extent to which the economic crisis and expenditure on ceremonial functions severely lower household expenditure on health and negatively influence health. Such analysis must be practicable and should assist in the learning of further critical knowledge and skill. Health professional students need to understand new financial plans, health system policy reforms, international cooperation, etc., to enable them to effect changes in expenditure patterns and to strengthen the welfare of society, as also suggested by the analysis of the social system.

The main focus of the second area of learning is the need to have a true picture of resources utilization. This requires development of the health professionals' skills not only in examining health budgets, but also skills in reducing or avoiding waste. This is because of, among other things, increasing health spending resulting from technological innovation and ever-more costly drugs. As treatments become available, people naturally want them and doctors want to prescribe them.

Accordingly, the common curriculum must stress the application of the principles of cost-efficiency and cost-benefit analysis. Such content must cover the things that are part of the health professional's daily work as well as other economic issues, such as financial management, the inequitable distribution of community resources and reward systems for health services, which are also reflected by the analysis of the social system. The accommodation of these content areas in the common curriculum must be based on a sound knowledge of economic concepts like balance of payments, supply and demand, imports and exports, markets etc. Students should also understand and be able to apply relevant basic mathematical and statistical concepts.

Communication System

We can see from the analysis of the communication system that in a particular country each of the many ethnic groups has its own language. However, due to social changes there is a common use of different languages across ethnic groups, with English being the official language in many African countries including the Gambia.

There are obviously two areas one can pick up from this for inclusion in the common curriculum: (1) the need for understanding the local languages, and (2) the necessity of extending the scope of English language teaching for the purpose of communicating vital health information.

While it may be desirable for health professionals to learn the language of all the people they serve, it will be impracticable to accommodate this in the common curriculum. The issue of language in a country where there are so many ethnic groups, as the analysis of the communication system in the previous chapter shows, is always bound to be tricky. Perhaps the most that the common curriculum can and should do is to provide opportunities for developing skills in the use of area languages and repute for respecting the language customs of the various ethnic groups. But there should be no doubt as to the importance of developing the English language skills of the health professional to be able to make available information to the right people at the right time andin a form that is easy to understand and use. The poor use of health information is an area of major weakness in the health systems of many developing countries. In general, although information is available centrally it is not being made available for planning or management at any other level. As has been mentioned, there is need for the use of both spoken and written English language more effectively, not only in our schools but also in public and private institutions, including health care institutions. Also the evidence suggests that the gap-filling exercise should go beyond this need for providing opportunities for developing understanding of the wider use of English language as a means of communication. It should include teaching in ways of exploring language to effect change. For example, Gordimer (1998) opposes the attitude of writers who make every effort to disestablish themselves: "not to be morally useful to the community". Gordimer suggests that the responsibility of the writer is to cause the audience, the reader to be astonished at the circumstances under which he or she was living and functioning. This is the basis of what is known as our protest literature. As Gordimer says, "whatever is written, with whatever purpose, whether to express the struggle for freedom, or the passion of a love affair, can only reach the power of truth in the measure in which the writer is capable of exploring the splendour of language brought to its services..."

The use of language in skilful ways to create an impact is not new as this article "The Making of an Empire" (Reid 1997) demonstrates:

...By the middle of the first century BC Rome was a cesspool of political intrigue and civic turmoil.

People waited eagerly for each new report from afar. Ceasar, who could write as skilfully as he fought, turned the composition of military dispatches into an art form. The triumph of his genre was his immortal message back to Rome after trouncing the Parthia's at Zeal in 47 BC: " Veni, vidi, vici – I came, I saw, I conquered ".

This was one of the greatest dispatches from the front in all military history. Indeed, because of the importance of such writing techniques, anthropologists are writing theses on the sociolinguistics of technologies such as electronic mail, thereby exploring the suggestion that social power is linguistic power in dormant communities. In other words, if one communicates clearly, people will take more notice of what one says.

Clearly, all these suggest the need for stressing in the common curriculum development of the English language skills of health professionals in both written and spoken English through strategies,such as giving English attention in students' written work, like project reports, and encouraging students to develop their English language proficiency by reading and participating in debates, etc.

Strategies that are useful for strengthening mastery of the English language must also be stressed: (1) the reading of recommended books, paying attention to the author's style, diction and syntax; (2) working on ones vocabulary by, for instance, searching the meaning of words in a dictionary; and (4) studying grammar, knowing the meaning of adverbs and adjectives, and to be able to recognize these in every part of speech and its function; practising spellings and mastering punctuation and capitalization.

There is also a need to emphasize in the common curriculum specialized kinds of language used in health care. These include scientific language such as mathematical and statistical symbols, diagrams and charts to communicate critical health information. Also opportunities for developing the health professionals computer language knowledge and understanding to store and retrieve, process and analyze, and use vital information, using computer software such as MEDLINE, EPI-INFO and the INTERNET (through which networks such as e-medicine that provides health workers in rural areas vital health information from urban areas for diagnostic purposes, for example, is channelled), must be provided in the common curriculum.

Other kinds of communication studies that have particular relevance for, particularly health education and promotion must also be given adequate coverage in the common curriculum. These include aspects of the mass media like film, advertising, radio and television, illustrated media to convey health massages, print media, songs with health messages, books, manuals, etc. The knowledge and understanding to be developed in these areas should not be limited to the understanding and use of such communication tools but must include ability to, where possible, produce them locally to be relevant to local cultures and needs, and must be basically national such as health education projects implemented in developing countries that may combine radio drama, detailed information to strengthen the radio programme and a cartoon magazine to enhance knowledge of immunization, etc. The use of traditional communicators like griots is also important and must be explored.

There is a final contradiction in the communication system that has important implications for the common curriculum, which must take us back to an earlier discussion. As the analysis shows, though the mass media is proving to be an important part of the communication system in developing countries, the majority of Gambians, for example, cannot always receive required health information through sources like radio and TV because of unaffordability of the cost of such resources and the lack of ownership and control of broadcasting stations and broadcasting programmes to rural communities. The consequences of this are indeed far-reaching. For example, the head of the AIDS programme in the Gambia, in stressing the need for a health education policy for the country, mentioned what he said is often a source of health educators' frustrations: "we say one thing; the media say a different thing." The curriculum proposals made with respect to especially the analysis of the social and economic systems in terms of inter and intra-sectoral collaboration, health policy, the reward system, expenditure patterns, and distribution of community resources are applicable here. In addition, to help secure the requirements of effective communication in health care such as increased computer access, the health professionals' skills of negotiation, mediation, advocacy, co-operation in a group, or with other groups, influencing health policy, effecting changes in the rewardsystem and expenditure patterns, must be used for tackling the critical social, political and economic problems that are inherent in the communication system, with a view to ensuring that the resources necessary for inputs needed for accessible vital health information are available and used effectively.

Rationality System

For the purpose of selecting from the rationality system it is also necessary to return to a point made earlier: the importance given to science with respect to the social and rationality systems has tended to have a prejudice against value and belief systems on health and illness and to conceal the necessity of comprehending other forms of reasoning and assessing what is applicable to cultural experiences like morality.

While it may be important to emphasize scientific thinking in the common curriculum, the various ways of thinking and feeling about health and diseases in communities must also be given adequate coverage. For example, the western biomedical model is sharply different from the concept of health and disease of, for instance, rural and traditional African communities where, as the analysis suggests, the germ theory has little or no importance. Consequently, people tend not to have much interest in prevention or modern treatment, as shown by the seemingly unwise behaviour of neglecting symptoms, not following a doctor's treatment, or not taking treatment at all. The experience to be provided must include development of the health professionals' understanding of such ideas and behaviour to deserve repute in the cultural context to justify attention instead of impulsive rejection.

Even the scientific thinking taught must consider such a complex and dynamic context. In the past three decades or so, social science researchers presumed that facts obtained from research could alone be sufficient basis for rational decisions for health development. But the results of the introduction of primary health care and the changes in the health systems following such introduction, such as growing community participation in decision-making, decentralization, the sharing of roles between men and women, etc., are increasingly making social development, including health development in particular a complicated process. This highlights the need for stressing in the common curriculum not only more extended research, but also new kinds of Interdisciplinary research, and understanding of the appropriate relationship between research, application of research, and involvement of communities in research, particularly social science research. A good example is applied health research that employs an anthropological approach which is characterized by, among other things, identification of the cultural factors that are associated with a problem. This approach must also provide understanding of how the health problems identified are connected with the different aspects of a country's health systems. The health professional's knowledge and skills in carrying out or participating in research in these areas such as equitable distribution of resources, community involvement, inter-sectoral co-operation, integration of serviceswithin the health system, participation of the private sector, etc, must be fully developed in accordance with his role and functions at the various levels of the health system so that he will be able to help bring about the needed changes.

It is reasonable to suggest that while it would be nice to increase peoples' knowledge on science, the majority of people, especially people in developing countries, will always comprehend very little of it. One reason for this is that many scientific facts are provisional, disputed, arcane and frankly unintelligible to anyone without higher mathematics. Therefore, a better approach would be to teach the methods of science without drowning people in detail, such as trying to compile and teach a list of compulsory facts. People in developing countries especially need some feel for how science strives to discover what is true and what is false. Although to train a scientist it is often still necessary to move through the traditional linear fashion through the details of the relevant discipline, however, for the layman, who will always need an interpreter to keep abreast of new discoveries, some familiarity with the scientific method is at least a way to keep the interpreters honest. A person thus equipped should be able to make sense of the claims by those who invoke science in debates over, for instance, the environment, abortion and public health (Hardon 1995)

The above discussion suggests two curricular options: one for the professional scientist and the other for the layman, together with content that will enable students appreciate the limitations of scientific rigour and the need for alternative approaches. These should be important components of the education of health professionals for the community. The degree, to which the former option, in particular, can or should be covered in the common curriculum, must be open to debate in teachers' curriculum planning, which is the subject of the next three chapters. This suggests another area of learning which the common curriculum must address. As we have already seen, there is a problem of not making information available for planning at the different levels of, for example, The Gambia's health care system. This requires development of the health

professional's knowledge and skills, in cultivating the needed support for establishing some degree of national research capability. Such research ability is perhaps best achieved in research and training centres which can bring participants in a field practice area from colleges, coupled with technical training in, for example, epidemiological methods, statistical concepts and the operation of

health services. The teaching of the content areas and strategies that can equip the health professional with the required knowledge and skills to use research information more effectively, some of which have been identified in relation to this and other systems, is also probably best conducted in research and training centres. The aim of such learning must include overcoming the barriers to effective use of research. This includes mobilization of interest groups, incorporating policy- makers on scientific advisory committees, etc., collating various research results, improving research methods and using the mass media; negotiating time by employing prompt phases of research; recruiting people who are able to translate science for the public and policy-makers, and organizing meetings between researchers and policy-makers for the purpose of presenting research results and to create mutual understanding and confidence between the parties concerned. Measures also include designing research that clearly specifies concrete and identifiable problems, and are designed to respond to specific programme interests; training in participation; transparency and fulfilment of anticipated needs, and commitment and seriousness on the part of senior management and inter-governmental review bodies to use the results of research effectively (e.g., Walt 1994) Besides, ethical considerations in research (a relationship with the morality system, especially) must be an important topic in the common curriculum. In particular, the main principles of beneficence (e.g., the protection of subjects from physical and psychological harm), respect for human dignity and justice, must be inculcated in students. This educational need has been highlighted by, for example, the 5th Human Genome Conference held in Windhoek, Namibia, in February 1999 (UNESCO 1999). During the conference a participant argued that there is a widening gap between genetic research and primary health care which should be addressed. While this argument received some approval from participants, mainly on the basis of ethical considerations with respect to commercial exploitation of rural communities on the use of blood samples for genetic research, apparently many could not see the relevance for or possibility of involving rural communities in highly scientific and technical research activities or issues like genetic counselling. This suggest that many health professionals still need to understand fully the principles of relevant conventions, such as the Declaration on the Human Genome and Human Rights (UNESCO 1997), to consider such principles important and to know how to put them in practice.

Technology System

The analysis of the technology system suggests three main points which can be the basis for selecting content here. One is that the technology that the common curriculum must emphasize should not mean technology that is inaccessible with regard to finance, safety, intellectual, value, feasibility and relevance in terms of the majority of the world's communities. This suggests that not only should health professionals return to basics but they must also utilize basic technology to their full advantage.

There are several descriptions of the use of simple technology in health care which illustrate this point, such as the use of a simple management information system to help Community Health Workers (CHWs) recognize the problem of malnutrition and to take effective action in the Katchi Abadis (squatter settlements) of Karachi, Pakistan (Aga Khan Foundation 1988):

...A management information system tracts the activities of the CHWs: which houses they should visit, who is at risk, and what is being done. The MIS tells where they are succeeding and where they are falling short and this information is fed back to them...

...A field staff person designed a simple map to put on the wall of a health centre, one for each CHW, with her assigned houses marked out. Coloured pins were stuck into the map, denoting the malnourished children. Every seriously malnourished child was indicated by a red pin. The CHWs visit the homes with the red pins frequently, sometimes daily. They have come to identify the homes with the red pins…

…We know that our MIS was working when a Baluch CHW, an illiterate but dependable woman who wears a burkha that hides all but her eyes, marched into the health centre one day, snatched a red pin out of the map, throw it on the floor, stamp on it and raised her head, eyes flashing. This was a small victory that she and a mother had won for one tiny child…

While this scene could take place in any other developing country, and while the lesson learnt from it may be applicable to such countries, for the sake of specificity in selecting content, however, it is necessary to draw from the previous analysis. Let us take, for example, the radio (and television) which, as mentioned before, is and will undoubtedly remain the commonest resource of communication, particularly for the rural communities of the Gambia, despite the present problem of people not able to afford the cost. Although radio and television have been around for a long time and more people have access to them, they have not been fully used as resource for education, management, or teaching. To fill this gap, the common curriculum must provide for development of interpersonal skills needed for assisting rural people relate to radios and to see the benefit of possessing them. It is also important for the health professional to be able to influence the use of radio through skills of negotiation and discussions to provide basic adult education in rural areas. This is vital to the rural person's appreciation and wellbeing and is a beneficial use of such a simple technology. One way through which such a technology can be used to be of maximum benefit to rural communities is to ensure that community members feel responsible for their own information. Therefore, the technology should be a means by which gaps between the rich and the poor, and the educated and uneducated, are narrowed, and to make people appreciate their crucial role in social development. This in short means the effective use of appropriate technology which, as mentioned in Chapter one, is one of the five principles of PHC.

The second point which clearly relates to the first point concerns the effectiveness and efficacy of appropriate health technologies. Jequier (1981) suggests that although the achievements in appropriate technology are notable, it must be borne in mind that "the problems appropriate technology pose are at least as numerous as the problems it was intended to solve". He listed as first of the new constraints the large divide between expectations and achievements. He gave several reasons for this gap in innovation. One is the length of time needed to translate sound ideas into a practically efficient technology. The second reason is that not only is it technically difficult to produce new low-cost technologies, it is equally problematic to make such technologies available to large numbers of people who need them. The third reason is that technologies relate to areas of permanent social and cultural activities of beneficiaries that are often controlled by constraining socio-cultural factors: religious taboos, norms and values, etc. Thus, it has been suggested by, for example, Jequier that though a large portion of expenditure and effort on appropriate technology is directed toward research and development in connection with equipment and collective production and transmission of information, the main demand that should be satisfied is the development of financial incentives, cultural knowledge, management, and legal structures that influence the outcome of the efforts at development and diffusion of appropriate technology. That while many countries are directing lots of money to research and development on technologies, such efforts have more significance than using technologies effectively. It seems that generally the creation and initially commercial exploitation of new products and processes are of more importance than the widespread and extensive use of appropriate technologies. The implications of this for the common curriculum have been dealt with in selecting from specifically the communication system. As has been mentioned, in order for the health professional to be able to provide or influence decision on the provision of modern communication, like microcomputer technology, the common curriculum must provide the student opportunities for development of not only relevant social skills, but also pertinent skills in economics, and especially politics, including legislation and policy-making. For while the technology idea has been supported by important persons in the industrial and financial sectors, the principal stumbling blocks that remain are political, rather than technical. The fundamental political options chosen by national governments are among the basic causes in the direction of the technological system (Jequier 1981).

This brings up the third related point which is the need for covering evaluation research on appropriate technology in the common curriculum. The new kind of managerial technology which is now required, but which is just appearing in the innovation scene of appropriate technology, are ideas like quality control, cost effectiveness, efficiency, safety, etc, as highlighted by several studies. (e.g, Berth 1996). The gap-filling action here is to include in the common curriculum content that will develop the knowledge and skills of the health profession to be able to assess the possible risks of technology used in health care (as noted also in relation to the rationality system) and to compare them with the likely benefits. While health professionals may not require the skills of a civil engineer, for example, it is advisable to provide them with the knowledge that will enable them to understand the hazards technologies used in health care can cause and to be able to evaluate the dangers of such technologies to the whole population.

In developing countries like the Gambia, an ideal starting point for the focus of the teaching of technology is to question whether the Gambia, for example, can develop a health technology that suits its needs. However, the teaching of health technology assessment like the teaching of social research described in relation to the rationality system can focus on the health system and programmes exploring the problems at the different levels. And because policy decisions are now often based on the technology used, the common curriculum should also make it possible for the health professional to, as we have already mentioned, develop knowledge and understanding on how to ensure that such research influences policy.

Morality System

Countries are generally multiethnic and moral pluralistic societies, with moral thinking based mainly on religion. This is especially true for many African countries where religion, particularly Islam, has a strong hold on peoples' lives, including their health. Yet many health professionals in these countries lack sufficient understanding of the religious principles on topics about health and the host of traditional norms and values that rest on such principles. While it may be impossible or undesirable to provide education on all the various aspects of morality as they relate to different religions or ethnic groups, sufficient time must be provided for exploration of the moral and ethical questions with health relevance.

As the analysis of the social system shows, there are misconceptions of, for example, Islamic principles on the role and status of women and children in society. The health professional requires adequate knowledge of the value systems that are based on Islamic principles, for instance, and the practices and beliefs that affect the health of especially women and children, such as early marriage, Female Genital Mutilation, unequal distribution of resources, etc. The teaching must also provide sound knowledge and understanding on the interaction between the traditional principles and the principles of relevant conventions, such as the conventions on The Rights of The Child and conventions for the Elimination of all forms of discrimination against women. This will in turn require good understanding of the legal system and legal processes, including how judicial powers, especially religious laws, are exercised. This teaching should equip the health professional with the knowledge that he can use to influence the legislative process in favour of women, children, as well as other vulnerable groups, and for carrying out or participating in sensitization programmes on health hazards and practices like female genital mutilation, artificial milk products, etc, which have been focal points of the discussion on the social and communication systems. It is crucial that ethical considerations in the formulation of control measures against these and other threats to health and well-being be afforded due emphasis in the common curriculum. Also, opportunities must be provided for gaining better insight into ethical dilemmas that come up in practical situations that are conditioned by culture and history. The health professional must be able to consider both what is likeable and what is feasible, for example, how to weigh the needs of society with that of an individual with regard to dealing with people living with HIV/AIDs.

There are two other ethical implications for the common curriculum. One is an ethical consideration with respect to legislation on education and practice of health workers. The common curriculum must include sufficient understanding for the variety of written and unwritten rules that traditional healers and health professional are subject to. The teaching must cover knowledge about the setting and use of technical and ethical standards/regulations, proposed guidelines and codes of good practice. Moreover, the promotion, dissemination and interchange of information on ethical issues and how to cooperate with all the people involved, using an honest and humane approach, must also be the foci of the teaching and learning.

These points to another related implication for the common curriculum, which should actually be the starting point in the selection. This is the need to include cultural dimensions as a basic component of the curriculum to promote mutual cultural understanding. The needs of learners (and patients/clients) must adequately be prepared for in the future through focusing attention on ethnographic views concerning learning and health care. This is because the aim of PHC in a radically pluralist world is to create a moral global environment in which the right to speak antagonistic moral languages, or express belief, or behave differently, and to actually hear each other, rather than to make one value win out over another value.

Belief System

As we noted in our analysis of the belief system, a country's belief system is similar to the morality system in that it is pluralist and is influenced strongly by religions. However, there are principles and values which all or most people living in a country seem to have in common, while other principles and values tend to be relative. One important aspect of the value system that seems to be disputable is democracy. The contradiction here is that although many countries are striving to be democratic societies, the provision of health care (or the resources for health) is not equally distributed to the people who need such care. Clearly, the way to fill this gap is to stress in the common curriculum content what will enable the student to inculcate values like fairness, social justice and respect for human rights (which have been stated in connection with the morality and rationality systems). The principles of "Health for all" and of PHC and community health, which embody such values, provide a common value system that can create opportunities for stimulating a series of new ideas and models of educating health professionals with the knowledge and understanding necessary for them to serve as real providers of PHC.

Although the belief system is generally pluralistic in many countries, there are seemingly some shared beliefs that appear as cultural differences with serious implication for health. Religious and magical beliefs which, as we have seen, are perhaps the most important often reject the biomedical concept of disease, a situation which leads to patients seeing doctors late for medical attention, a feeling of lack of control over one's life, helplessness, etc. These beliefs are often mistakenly assignable to stupidity or ignorance. The gap-filling exercise here must include learning that will develop in students the values we mentioned earlier- to respect such beliefs and behaviour, not to attribute them to ignorance or stupidity, and to know how to deal with them in a proper manner in particular situations. Because traditional beliefs and behaviour place traditional healers on first-line care, experiences planned for the education of the health professional should, as indicated earlier, be integrated with that of the health and social systems with which they operate. This will help the student acknowledge the importance of such traditional beliefs and ways of acting, and to develop reputation for regarding traditional healers and other health workers as important members of the multidisciplinary health team.

Aesthetic System

While an exploration of the confusion in the aesthetic systems of countries in terms of the nature and range of aesthetic experiences may be difficult, such an exploration can be useful for selecting content for the common curriculum. As the analysis in the previous chapter shows, there are both traditional and modern forms of art and entertainment that are ascribed, for instance, to the majority of people living in a country and to those living in the urban and peri-urban areas of the country, respectively. However, there are commonalities in terms of aesthetic experiences across ethnic groupings and locations, as is the case in other systems, such as the social system. The selection here must therefore stress what is good for and is applicable to the majority of the people in a country that can be used in efforts at improving their health and welfare. When this approach is used, it will be seen that both simple and complex aesthetic experiences deserve aesthetic attention, with perhaps the simple experiences necessarily gaining more importance because they are the categories most frequently employed by rural people, particularly in developing countries, in relation to their cultural activities – language and communication, religious beliefs, marriages, family and sexual relationships, psychological issues, etc.

Some examples to illustrate these points: For one example, we must return to the selection from the communication system. As outlined there, a health education project (Butt et al 1997) incorporating drama, radio and a cartoon magazine has been used to reinforce knowledge about immunization.

Another example where songs with health messages and illustrated print media were combined to convey health education and promotion shows that simple aesthetic experiences are excellent to be worthy of attention in the common curriculum. An example of the use of excellent and complex or modern aesthetic experiences in health care is a non- traditional health education/promotion approach (Silayan-Go 1990) developed to help decrease pregnancy among Filipino teenagers. It consisted of two popular recorded songs with a cautionary message about young love as a backdrop of educational and support activities, featuring a telephone hot- line staffed by experienced counsellors.

There are also examples of the use of aesthetic experiences in order to effect social change, a strategy that should also be an important topic in the common curriculum. One example drawn from an article entitled "An Esthetic of Outrage" (Newsweek 1997) concerns photojournalism on the plight of landless peasants in Brazil:

"The 52-year-old Salgado who, as a youth, saw the small farms of his hometown of Aymore's gobbled up by land barons, knows these problems well and now, as an acclaimed documentary photographer based in Paris, he has the attention of a world-wide audience. Salgado's new book 'Terra' (Phaidon Press), is a collection of 100 photographs taken between 1980 and 1996. They depict the plight of the homeless, the jobless and the hopeless of Brazil- 'people wandering between dreams and despair'"- in the words of Jose Saramago, the impassioned Portuguese writer whose text accompanies Salgado's images. Salgado plans to launch the book in Europe, the United States and Latin America.

...Last week Salgado was again at the barricades. His Brazilian book tour and roving picture exhibition was planned to coincide with a march by peasant demonstrators and supporters into Brasilia to decry the country's lopsided land structure. "Brazil is the only country with a movement willing to look to the country side for solutions", Salgado told the applauding students. The TV crews and print photographers were there to record every word. But Salgado, never one to miss a moment, rose to his feet, grabbed his Leica [camera] and snapped off a few frames. Just for the record…"

Another example on photojournalism from a local paper with the caption "Photoscope: Threats to Environmental Health" is equally interesting. It presents several photographs of private and public places, each with a relevant statement focusing attention on the public health significance of a poor environmental condition and the need for action, for example, "A factory with pollution coming out of it. Any way to tackle it?". "Children collecting soda elements from the gutter behind the factory. Is it safe for them?". "Rice fields and palm trees suffering environmental onslaught. Who will speak for them?"
One cannot help but remember the saying: "A picture is worth a thousand words." Many studies are now looking at the patients' need of aesthetic means of expression for their well-being and recovery to health. Several of these research areas emphasize the patient's preferences for views containing trees and other vegetation (e.g., Day 1990, Ulrich 1986a, Ulrich 1986 b). They found that the benefits of visual encounters with vegetation were significant for individuals experiencing stress or anxiety. Hospital window views influence patients' feelings positively and accordingly affect recovery from surgery. Rubin (1998) reported a relationship between environmental design and patients' medical outcome. For example, furniture placement had a positive impact on patients during hospital treatment. Humour is acknowledged as an important psychological variable with a wide range of effects. For instance, Bullock (1983) who examined the effect of humour on anxiety in children, found that children exposed to humorous material had a significantly lower state of anxiety compared to children exposed to non-humorous material. Various studies suggest that music can help patients to deal with pain which is the most common complaint among patients that demands nursing attention. Locsin (1981), for example, studied the effect of music on the pain of post-operative patients and found significant differences between a control and experimental sample in their verbal pain reactions with a positive impact in the music group. In a controlled intervention study, reproductions of works of art were used as communication tools with elderly women. A positive life perception was found in the art group compared to the control group (Wikstro̎m 2000). Cohen (1993) suggests that the therapeutic use of literature can be invaluable in helping a patient to understand and cope with illness, because the patients tend to see their life situations in the books they read. Reading can also be used as a spring-board to

nurse–patient discussions. Knowledge of how such aesthetic means of expression play a vital role in patients' recovery processes should be included in the common curriculum. The aesthetic experiences selected must however be culturally appropriate.

Summary

In summary, this chapter has shown that it is important to stress in the common curriculum knowledge of the significance of personal values, beliefs in health care and enhance students' understanding of the importance of sociocultural factors in disease prevention. This must be accompanied by relevant applied science and mathematics, including psychosocial science and political science. The common curriculum should include people's moral thinking and feeling about health and diseases. The delivery of PHC that is meaningful, acceptable, accessible, effective and cost –effective demands a better understanding of the socio-cultural backgrounds of patients and clients, their families and the environment in which they live. It is crucial to have a good knowledgeof how peoples' cultural values, beliefs and assumptions influence the care provided and are formed by social relationships and the context in which health workers live and work. This chapter has further demonstrated that the eight systems of cultural analysis are closely interrelated. For example, the social, communication and technology systems are clearly connected to each other and to the aesthetic system in terms of the kinds of communication and technology aspects that can be used in both simple and complex aesthetic experiences to tackle socio-cultural issues in health care. Pertinent knowledge on these should be important parts of the common curriculum. As in the communication and technology systems, the effective use of simple and complex or modern aesthetic experiences in health care require inter and intra-sectoral collaboration and pertinent decision and actions with respect to health policy, reward systems, expenditure patterns, distributionof resources, etc. The learning in such areas must also be an important component of the common curriculum. The discussion will turn in the following chapters to consideration of the business of making comparisons of the eight systems with the content of current courses/subjects in health professional education, and of knowing how the existing subjects or courses could be strengthened or augmented by additional subjects in order to create a more inclusive common curriculum. But first let us look in the next chapter at the influences and constraints that will have a bearing on such curriculum planning.

7

The Context of Curriculum Planning

While there may be differences between the health professions and even between countries, managers of health educational institutions, like all other managers, specify their roles in terms of the expectations of those who have importance for them. The manager must reckon with many people and agencies in curriculum planning and curriculum innovation. In this chapter we shall focus on the influences and constraints outside as well as inside education that operate on curriculum planning (Kelly 1982), including how the examination system affects curriculum planning and curriculum innovation. Such influences may be interconnected and conflicting, straightforward and indirect, visible and secret, intentional and incidental. In doing this, we shall look especially at the origins of difficulties in and outside health professional educational institutions. It is necessary to know these influences and constraints at the beginning, in order not to view curriculum planning as a simple business of the use of logic and rationality, a point that is an important perspective of this book. The chapter shall consider the important issues of accountability and evaluation, which are the major features of attempts at the control of curriculum. It is crucial that the chapter includes understanding of the various facets of this strong influence on curriculum planning. Accountability and evaluation of the curriculum- extremely complex and political concepts in which evaluation (and accountability) can serve as a mere activist, whose main aim is to improve an educational situation, an arbitrator seeking to reconcile the divergent interests, an onlooker whose only usefulness is his inert presence, a rider's prodding whip, or a deadly weapon. But first the chapter shall concentrate on a powerful context for learning, the community, which stimulates deep learning and should be a critical consideration when planning physical and virtual learning spaces in community - oriented education for health professionals.

The Community

Here, the term community means the social context of students and their environments. A community is a group of people with a common purpose, shared values, and agreement on goals and therefore has powerful qualities that condition learning. A community has the power to motivate its members to exceptional performance. Conditions that matter for student success in a community have been described as commitment by community members to communicating with one another on an ever deeper and more authentic level, setting standards of expectation for the individual and providing the climate in which great things can materialize (Kuh et al 2005). In higher education such communities are characterized as research communities, learning communities and communities of practice. Learning is often equated with the acquisition of facts and skills by students, which in a community are enriched by factors such as mentorship, encouragement, and an understanding of the viewpoints and distinctive qualities of a growing different membership.

While learning has to do with individual behavioural changes, the context in which those changes occur is a social environment involving many people. Thus all components of education such as the planning of space design should consider community. Social interactions play a critical role in facilitating learning and improving student engagement: through community. Because of the critical roles that physical and virtual learning spaces play in influencing community, it is important that educators look again at the role of virtual and physical space as a way to improve student (as well as faculty and staff) learning and engagement in community.

There are two primary reasons why society should care about learning in community (Boyer et al 1996). One is that learning is a social process that works best in a community setting, thus yielding the best use of societal resources. Learning theories, especially social cognitive learning theory, argue for a rich environment in which students and faculty share meaningful experiences that go beyond the one-way information flow characteristic of typical lectures in traditional classrooms. The other reason is that learning in community will have an important part to play in preparing students for their work-life to come. Graduates of professional training institutions, for example, must succeed in professional environments that require interactions with other people. Due to the volatility of information today and the increase of information flow, community-based education will help prepare graduates to live and work in a world that requires greater collaboration Community has always been an intended foundation of higher education. In the past higher education in Western countries occurred at community-centered institutions. As we mentioned in a following section, early universities and colleges were private, residential, and almost exclusively connected to a religious founding organization. This fostered civic engagement among student and staff, and others within the learning environment.

However, today learning in community is decreased due to several factors. One is that expansion of large public institutions to accommodate government-mandated support of larger enrolments, leading to the emphasis of efficiency in structuring processes and to larger class sizes. The fixed costs of universities from the high proportion of labour result in the cost of attending college rising faster than inflation. The result of this is the creation of pressures for cost-cutting by increasing class sizes, for instance. There are other factors that have increased the loss of community. They include increasing demands on faculty for research productivity outside the classroom, increasing numbers of commuter students, and an increasingly secularized society. These factors have contributed to the erosion of the social interactivity that characterized the earlier model of higher education based on the Western system. As classrooms became larger during the mid-20th century, the level of social interaction decreased within the classroom, making the role of the student in the teaching and learning process increasingly that of a scribe. The sense of community within higher education has become increasingly concealed, a situation that has negative consequences for both students and faculty. A result of this is that the lack of interactivity lessens students' expectations for their educational experience (Graff 2003). Another is that it adds to tension between a student culture and an academic culture (Bickford et al 2010). According to Bickford et al some commentators have observed an unspoken pact, which translates to faculty not expecting much of students so that they can concentrate on the growing demands of research, and students not demanding rigorous instruction so that they can concentrate on their social lives.

Today, students who are increasingly connected devote less and less time to structured, instruction-driven learning. It is therefore proper to look again at the role of community as a way to improve student, faculty, and staff engagement and learning. Chapter 10 on managing the curriculum innovation and change considers how community of learning can be used to foster the education and training of healthcare professionals in the community.

Tradition

History or tradition is another influence that affects decisions about the health care educational institutions that we must consider. Head teachers and their teachers have been schooled in certain ways with regard to the subject they teach and the teaching methods they use, which are difficult to change. Doing so will mean that they will have to begin all over again- to learn new ways of teaching and forgo the confidence which teaching a subject provides, or using certain techniques with which they feel secure and in which they are sure of their knowledge and capability. Tradition encouraged specialists to attend to their individual areas, such as teachers developing pedagogy and curriculum; information technologists making decisions about technology; and facilities managers designing and developing classrooms and other spaces. Too often, the academic and professional worlds are marked by vocationalism, the fragmentation of knowledge, and territoriality (Boyer et al 1996). This, to a large extent, seemingly accounts for the resistance to organizational change.

As will be seen in the following chapter, we have stressed the need for the provision of the kind of continuing education that will enable teachers to initiate and conform to organizational change. We have also emphasized the need for other measures that can facilitate or motivate the introduction and sustenance of change. Throughout this discussion, the main focus is the teacher who is placed at the centre of the curriculum planning stage. It is not surprising, therefore, that when we consider the influence of history and tradition; we must necessarily do so with particular reference to the teacher and his profession.

Professional Standards

The fact that the teacher lies at the heart of any best curriculum planning effort also requires that we consider how he is influenced by his profession. Such influence finds expression in several ways. For example, efforts at ensuring that educational programmes are relevant to the health needs of the population may be frustrated by the traditionalism of educators, often supported by reference to some obscure professional standards.

The two fundamental intentions in the regulation of nursing education, for instance, are standard-setting and administration (ICN 1989) Standard setting involves making sure that there are basic definitions of nursing and deciding upon qualifications for education. Administration includes explaining these standards, developing mechanisms and tools for executing them and carrying out the real processes of regulation. These two functions find practical expressions in credentialing the nurse and in approving schools (ICN 1986). The intention is to tailor the scope of nursing practice to suit the ability of the nurse. Therefore, educational standards designated by law are viewed as having an important function in the development of the nursing profession.

According to an international study on nursing regulation (ICN 1986), while there may be diversity between countries in this respect, in terms of pre-nursing education and in the nursing programme itself, its content, setting and duration, in most countries the emphasis is on educational standards upon curriculum. Data from the study shows that subject matter takes on more importance in law than exposure to expert educators and role models, and arguably educational facilities and resources. The controlling of licensing or similar forms of examinations or, interchangeably, the acknowledgement of nursing school exams as adequate for registration is one important measure for judging the quality of the education provided. This stress on this form of monitoring of standards is underscored by the use of examination data by health professionals and employing authorities for the purpose of monitoring educational standards. Generally, health authorities have used the results of licensing and similar modes of exams as barometers for assessing the quality of the education of health professional without, acknowledging differences in local constraints with regard to other factors in the schools, such as the role of teachers and other educational facilities and resources. This limitation is highlighted by the cultural analysis framework that identifies a wide range of measures for purposes of evaluation. Thus, we will necessarily have to return to it in a following section that deals with accountability and evaluation, in Chapter 9 which describes evaluation models, and in Chapter 10 on the management of the curriculum innovation and change.

Government Policy/Political Ideology

Although the teaching profession, or other professions (e.g., nursing and medical professions) can influence teachers in their curriculum planning, the professions themselves can in turn be influenced by factors outside the school. One of such factors is government finance. Financial restraints resulting from government funding policy may render professional aspirations for curriculum development initiatives impossible, though they may at times support such aspirations. Decisions made by governments about the organization of schools may also conflict with or back professional aspirations, such as a policy that requires all medical education programmes in a country's institutions to follow the same curriculum plan, and curriculum review models suggested by Ministries of Health not agreeing with professional goals of university education for entry into practice.

As we shall see in the following chapters, this disagreement of forces gives the ideal foundation for change, as it facilitates the interaction of and the development of a balance between these two main pressures (government policy and professional aspirations) affecting education and curriculum change. This alone is enough justification for presentation of these two conflicting interests on convocational bodies for curriculum change (Kelly 1982).

There can be pressures exerted on schools by individuals and bodies responsible for funding and running schools at the local level of a country, which supposedly should make local governments have a lot of power. However, it must not be forgotten that the greater part of the money local governments spend on education is provided by central government in one form or another. Because of this central governments often put pressure on or direct curriculum planning.

The effects central government has on curriculum planning is clearly much greater in countries where serious decisions concerning the curriculum are made internally and where and when observance of orthodox rules is a demand for getting aid. Such effects are also exceedingly straightforward. Even if such control is not straightforward, decisions about the educational system made internally will have meaning for the curriculum. Where a country has a powerful governing political ideology, such as in the communist countries, prior to the break up of the Soviet Union, the curriculum will mirror greatly that political ideology.

Political Interest Groups

Though, in a more general way the curriculum is frequently influenced by the political ideology of a country, in all countries education is in the middle of the political arena. Additionally, political interest groups, apart from those linked to political parties, are created for the purpose of advancing particular types of educational change, or influence the growth of education globally. In health care the bodies that are clearly among such groups are the Medical Councils and Nurses and Midwives Councils, and the health professional associations or unions.

International Bodies

The procedures of international bodies are increasingly affecting governments and, consequently, the planning of education for health professionals. Some have argued that control over the policies of developing countries is increasingly being relinquished to international organizations; that the policies of developing countries are being driven externally by financial institutions like the World Bank. By means of the UN agencies and on the basis of relationships between nations, some nations can pressure other nations to reform systems of health and related education. The leading UN agencies like he United Nations Population Fund (UNFPA) in addition to being interested in health, can actually influence health, including the education of health personnel. Also, trans-national corporations, pressure groups and NGOs who operate in the international arena may also influence policy on health in general including the education of health personnel.

Religious Bodies

There are other bodies that were created for other purposes but are also involved in education and, consequently, participate in discussions about health professional education. The churches that have advanced the creation of education for health professionals in many countries are clearly the most influential. Not only do churches possess schools and colleges, they in addition exercise great influence by means of the education they provide for doctors, nurses etc, in the institutions they have created. In Chile, for example (The Economist1997), where the Catholic Church owns or runs one-in ten of privately-owned schools, the Church is influential in education from kindergartens to universities. Another example is Cuttington University College in Liberia, which is owned by the Episcopal Church of that country, and which offers degree courses in nursing. Even in a small country like The Gambia, Christianity and Islam have some influence on education through its schools, though not directly in the education of health professionals.

Economy

A country's economy is another very influential aspect on education. Often, it is economic events and factors that determine the development of most systems of education. The economic influences compel schools to stress in their curricula areas of study or content that is considered to have economic value. Therefore, for instance, there has been pressure on health training schools to stress in their curricula community health/PHC subjects. Usually, what matters is the extent to which educational programmes fulfil the economic criteria of cost-effectiveness and efficiency. In other words, "the benefits foregone from not being able to use the same resources in their best alternative use" (Drummond 1987). In the present financial strictness, such economic influences are exercised directly by judgments made regarding the allotment of money, resources, equipment, materials and staff to schools and colleges. However, related research (Hanushek, cited in the Economist 1997) has shown that there is little evidence that spending more money on education does make for better students. The report indicates that while money is needed for education, additional money does not unintentionally improve students' learning because, as the report says, having computers in every classroom, for example, may not infuse basic skills. The report goes on to say that the lesson here is to "spend money well, not prodigally" Mass Media

The influence of the mass media on the processes of health policy is usually underrated (Walt 1994). There are two kinds of mass media. One is the print media, consisting of newspapers, books, magazines, etc; the other, the electronic media, comprises films, television, radio, internet, etc. These aspects of communication are called 'mass media' because their communicative sphere of use or functions is very extensive indeed, and can cover a whole society, particularly in developed countries. In developing countries the influence of the media in policy making is not all that clear (Walt 1994). However, they can have many functions: they can facilitate the transmission of a society's culture; they can serve as information providers and tools for propaganda; and they can be used as instruments of genuineness, originating plurality of beliefs in, and approval of key economic, social and political organizations.

Walt argues that though the mass media can focus peoples' attention to issues, it is not likely to do so if the topic relates to 'low politics' issues. If the subject concerns 'high politics' issues that relate to a country's security, for example, it is probable that most of the media will back the essential government drives, provided the government is considered to be justifiable or genuine.

Accountability and Evaluation

Accountability, like evaluation, is a complex issue. Also, like evaluation accountability is a political matter. It is concerned with giving information on the success or failure of instructional provisions through various modes such as test results, to funders of such provisions. While each of these situations may be different in each situation a judgement is made on the performance of teachers, or learners, or the merits of the methods used. In addition, accountability deals with responsibility and recognizing that responsibility in a public way. Thus, accountability entails evaluation but evaluation does not necessary involve accountability. The two topics are outlined as follows:

Accountability

Generally, two main models of accountability can be identified. One is the bureaucratic model, also called utilitarian, instrumental or hierarchical model. The other is the professional, intrinsic or democratic model. The main features and inadequacies of each of these opposing models are outlined as follows:

1. Bureaucratic Model

Main features

The teacher is held accountable to the public who pays the tax that provides the resources the teacher uses; The main concern is achievements made for the money used; There is emphasis on the results of pre-specified objectives; The major ways of assessing the competence of teachers is student scores on standardized tests which the teacher conducts but does not write. Future provision of resources is dependent on the results of these tests.

Main Inadequacies

The acknowledgement of simple goals of education is encouraged by the suggestion that the only thing that can be measured can be taught; The teacher is given responsibility without freedom; The type of data given by such mode of accountability are not helpful in decision-making concerning how to improve the performance of individual schools or teachers for it does not show the factors that contribute to poor performance on the test, only that performance is poor.

2. Democratic Model

Main Features

The teacher is required to adhere to principles of practice instead of the outcomes manifested by student performance; It indicates the possibility of the use of the "process model" of curriculum planning, its basis being the acknowledgement that the value of education settles in the actual process of teaching-learning instead of the outcomes of evaluation.

Main Inadequacies

Difficulties of constructing appropriate and practicable schemes of accountability. As the above discussion shows, the kind of evaluation that the democratic model of accountability proposes cannot be the easy kind of summative measurement of student performance related to the bureaucratic model. It must be an illuminative kind of evaluation planned to give information for the different stakeholders and agencies, as can be seen from the following section on evaluation.

Evaluation

Evaluation connotes decisions about efficiency, the purpose of education, teaching methods, as well as the means of accumulating evidence and reaching conclusions on these bases. One dilemma is that evaluation is a complex and different process that needs professionalism. There are fairly seven kinds of evaluation which are required from time to time in most educational systems (Lawton 1983):

1. Estimates of pupil performance and/or competence.
2. Estimates of pupil competence at the terminal point of schooling.
3. Estimates of teacher's competence for different motives/ purposes including promotion.
4. udgments about the effectiveness of a school (or group of schools).
5. Ways/forms of providing useful information about teaching materials, including new curriculum projects.
6. The evaluation of diffusion or dissemination.
7. Judgments about validity/kind of process involved, for example, are what the pupil is learning, or the teacher trying to teach worthwhile?

As already mentioned and as this list suggests, there is much importance given to examinations in the evaluation of the educational preparation of students, including students of the health professions. Because examinations (written, oral, practical, or others) are often the principal means by which faculties gather information on the performance of students, it means that the testing programme would include examinations designed to (1) aid in selecting school applicants (aptitude tests); (2) assist in determining the appropriate placement of students in the sequence of courses comprising the school curriculum (proficiency or placement tests); and (3) yield a detailed profile of student and teacher to plan subsequent learning experiences that make the best use of educational resources (diagnostic examinations or formative evaluations); and (4) provide data essential to decisions about promotions, graduation, or licensure (certifying examinations or summative evaluation).

This shows the difficulties examinations pose on curriculum planning. One of such constraints is that the limitations of the schemes used for evaluation can result in narrowness in teachers' and students' educational goals. Another constraint is that there is inducement to plan curriculum to suit the schemes of evaluation used, which is clearly more likely to happen in connection with certifying examinations. This is because examinations are designed to sample each of the major elements in any unit of instruction, so that diagnostic testing can yield specific information about how much a student has learned and how much more he needs to learn. Furthermore, every element of content is further analyzed into the sub-tasks (a method used in specification of objectives) required for mastering that element, and each sub-task must be represented in the diagnostic examination on that unit, to make such testing provide data that are helpful in determining the cause of identifiable deficiencies. However, many teachers consider such public examinations major constraints to curriculum change, because as long as assessment of individual students is the method of evaluation, existing assessment schemes will continue to produce limitations to curriculum planning. Chapter 9 on organization of the common curriculum will consider alternative approaches to evaluation in relation to cultural analysis.

Summary

In the foregoing discussion in this chapter, several categorizations of interacting, but at times conflicting influences and constraints to curriculum planning are detectable. Such influences usually come from individuals or groups with different perspectives on schools and the curriculum. To begin with, a distinction is made between administrative and professional factors. As we have seen, both types inhibit and induce curriculum planning and are likely to disagree with one another. A distinction is made between national and local influences; those that function inside the school are differentiated from the influences that operate outside the school. It is important to realize that the factors that are identifiable will have different importance at various levels of health care systems. Besides, we must not forget that, in all of these, the influences will tend to at several stages be in disagreement with one another, thus making the type of curriculum change that will actually materialize the product of these several conflicting and competing powers. We must now turn to consideration of the curriculum planning which is influenced by the factors outlined above, and which curriculum planners must consider or deal with in their planning.

8

Planning for a Community-Oriented Common Curriculum: Curriculum Coverage

In discussing the planning of the common curriculum in schools, Lawton (1983) laid down general principles as a basis for interpreting guidelines into a working curriculum. Lawton also considered the problems of epistemology, including adequate coverage of the ground, and organization. The same approach will be followed here, but although the issues of coverage and organization are closely connected they will be discussed separately. This chapter will deal with curriculum coverage. Comparing Existing Subjects with what is required in Terms of the Eight Systems In looking at the problem of redesigning or revising an existing curriculum, or planning a new curriculum from the perspective of a health professional educational institution, let us, like Lawton (1983), use an imaginary and very conventional school, in this case, a nursing school. Because the school is so traditional, its curriculum is arranged on the basis of subjects that have distinct labels, as Table 9 shows.

Table 9: Existing Nursing School Subjects (Examples)

Basic Subjects
a. Physical and biological sciences (Phy)
b. Psychology (Psy)
c. Social Science (Soc)

Nursing Subjects
d. Nursing Fundamentals (History of Nursing, Ethics etc (Nurs)
e. Medical & Surgical nursing (Me)
f. Maternal and child health nursing (Ma)
g. Paediatric nursing (Pa)
h. Psychiatry nursing (Ps)
Others
i. Education (Ed)
j. Community Health (Co)
k. Management (Man)

Such a list of subjects may be defined in the school's regulations or chosen by the group of course planners. Table 10compares the listed subjects (examples) with content required in relation to the eight systems. Such a framework enables planners to begin the conversion to a cultural analysis kind of curriculum. But to cope with this complex matching process a technique that goes beyond such comparison is required (Lawton 1983). This is the curriculum matrix technique which is, fundamentally, a tool for comparing existing resources with a new condition, indicating gaps and possibly mismatches, and therefore improving the planning of courses.

Eight Systems

Table 10: Comparison of Existing Nursing School Subjects (examples) with Content required in Relation to the Eight Systems

	System	Existing Subjects (Examples)	New Subjects or topics needed (Examples)	Comment
1	Social	-Physical Science -Biological Science -Social Science -Nursing fundamentals -Medical & -Surgical nursing -Maternal and child health nursing -Paediatric nursing -Psychiatry nursing	-History of Nursing in The Gambia -Political concepts -Political skills -Lobbying, etc. -Health system -Health & other health-related teams -Management skills including Interpersonal skills, e.g., advocacy, negotiation etc.	Link with other systems

			-Motivation, rewards, etc. -Health policy analysis -Population and gender issues -Law and legal processes	
2	Eco-nomic	Community health Management	-Economic concepts -Health economic principles. -Macro and micro-economic analysis -Resource mobilization and utilization -Expenditure patterns -Budgets -Equity in resource allocation -Development economics -Financial Management including procurement, disbursement, etc. -Motivation, rewards	Link with other systems
3	Commu-nication System	Education Community health Fundamentals of Nursing	-Modern communication systems -Mass communication, print media -Film radio & TV studies -Ownership & control, -Legislation -Communication studies -Micro-technology & Health education -Health statistics & Computing -Computer studies -Distance learning -Internet, etc -Meetings, minutes, reports	Link with other systems

4	Rational-ity	-Physical and bio-logical sciences -Social sciences -Psychology -Nursing research	-Theoretical perspectives of nursing -Health Systems Research -Extended social science research -Anthropological methods -Statistical concepts, tools, etc. -Epidemiological studies -Biomedical and tradition-al ideas on health & dis-ease. -Multi-and interdiscipli-nary research teams. -Evaluation & use of research data -Management of research -Ethical considerations	Link with other systems
5	Technol-ogy	-Fundamentals of Nursing -Medical & Surgi-cal nursing -Maternal and child health nurs-ing -Paediatric nursing -Psychiatry nurs-ing	-Modern Nursing equip-ment and devices -Appropriate health technology -Micro-technology -Computer studies -Computer technology -Socio-cultural, economic and political factors influencing technology use -Problems of health technology production and diffusion -Simple and complex health technologies -Traditional medicine -Modern Pharmaceuticals -Technology assessment – effectively, efficiency, etc. -Ethical consideration	Link with other systems

6	Moral	-Fundamentals of Nursing -Sociology -Psychology	-Comparative religious Studies -Religious principles, conventions, laws, codes and health -Distinction between law & ethics. -PHC principles -Roles, status, rules, human rights & wellbeing -Moral, ethical questions & health -Related legislative processes -Control measures against threats to health & wellbeing	Link with other systems
7	Belief	-Fundamentals of Nursing -Sociology -Psychology -Community health	-Traditional belief systems & health -Science and health -Comparative religious studies -Political beliefs	Link with other systems
8	Aesthetic	-Sociology -Psychology -Fundamentals of Nursing -Community health	-Aesthetic experiences transferred to patient care: • Literature • Architecture • Nature experience • Theatre • Circus • Religion • Humour	Link with other systems

Adapted from Lawton (1983)

Curriculum Matrix Planning

It has been suggested (Lawton 1983) that a practical approach to curriculum matrix planning is to begin at a more general and encompassing level, as shown in Table 11, Matrix A, and then go on simplifying the process by matching subject proposals with the requirements of the common curriculum, based on the different course years for each aspect of Lawton's eight systems model.

Course planners should go on to construct syllabuses by charting the areas of knowledge/concepts, and probably, skills and attitudes to be dealt with during the course, then separating this content into three different years (for a 3-year State Registered Nurse (SRN) course).

Table 11: Matrix A

Purpose: to match existing subjects with the requirements of the new common curriculum and identifying gaps.

Existing Subjects (Examples)	a	b	c	d	e	f	g	h	i	j	k
Systems (including new subjects)	Phy	Psy	Soc	Nurs	Me	Ma	Pa	Ps	Ed	Co	Man

Social

(Psycho-Social concepts)

e.g status, roles and motivation)

(Applied Sociology)

(Applied Psychology)

(Social traditions, cultural patterns & health

(Motivation, rewards, etc.)

(Political concepts)

(Political skills, e.g lobbying, propaganda)

(Management concepts)

(Management interpersonal skills, e.g., advocacy, negotiation, etc).

(Health systems)

(Health & other Teams)

(Health policy analysis

(Population & Gender)

(Moral issues)

(Law and legal processes

Economic
(Economic concepts)
(Health economic principles)
(Macro and micro-economic analysis)
(Resource mobilization & utilization)
(Equity in resource allocation)
(Financial management)
(Development economics)
(Expenditure patterns)
(Budgets)
(Motivation, rewards, etc)

Communication
(Communication systems)
(Mass communication, print media)
(Film, radio & TV studies)
Ownership, control, legislation, etc)
(Communication studies)
(Advertisement, propaganda)
(Health education)
(Micro-technology)
(Health statistics & computing)
(Computer studies, Internet, etc)
(Distance learning)
(Art, entertainment, music, poetry)
(Meetings, minutes, reports)

Rationality
(Theoretical perspectives of nursing)
(Health system research)
(Extended social science research)
(Anthropological studies)
(Epidemiological methods)
(Statistical concepts, tools, etc.)
(Biomedical & traditional ideas on health & disease)
(Multi-and-interdisciplinary research teams)
(Evaluation of research & use of research data)
(Management of research)
(Evaluation, research and health policy)
(Ethical considerations)

Technological
(Nursing care procedures)
(Nursing equipment and devices)
(Appropriate health technology)
(Micro-technology)
(Computer studies)
(Socio-cultural, economic & political factors)
(Problems of health technology production & diffusion)
(Simple & complex health technologies)
(Traditional medicine)
(Technology assessment-effectiveness, efficiency, etc.)
(Ethical considerations)

Morality
(Applied social psychology)
(Comparative religious studies)
(Religious principles, conventions, codes, laws and health)
(Distinction between laws & ethics)
(PHC principles)
(Roles, status, rules, human rights and well-being, etc.)
(Moral, ethical questions & health)
(Related legislative processes)
(Promotion of mutual cultural understanding)
(Respect for peoples' customs & traditions)
(Control measures against threats to health & well-being)

Belief
(Traditional beliefs & health)
(Science & health)
(Comparative religious studies)
(Political beliefs)

Aesthetic
(Cultural activities & aesthetic experiences)
(Film, radio & TV studies & use)
(Health education)
(Art, music & entertainment)
(Literature)
(Architecture
(Photography)

(Nature experience)
(Theatre)
(Religion)
(Humour)
Adopted from Lawton (1983)

Therefore the sequence of events for a school staff could be (Lawton 1983):

1. Choose a curriculum model (or models) that can integrate curriculum elements or classify knowledge or experiences into a conceptually meaningful structure (e.g., Lawton's eight systems (Table 10) and the Integrated curriculum model (Chapter 3).

2. For each aspect of experience group of teachers (possibly with the help of experts) should engage in syllabus construction by identifying the knowledge, skills and attitudes to be included in the programme, then separating this content into three different years.

3. Producing a rough matching of existing subjects (and teachers) with the demands of the new curriculum (Table 11, Matrix A) This will indicate the deficiencies in content and the need for teachers who will be required to offer the new subjects/topics, such as political concepts.

4. After identifying main deficiencies in existing content, planners can then progress to more extensive matrix analysis. This involves matching every aspect of the curriculum, for each year, against subjects such as politics, as shown in Table 12, Matrix B.

Table 12: Matrix B.
Purpose: to match existing subjects (examples) with the requirements of the new Political subjects.

Subjects	Phy	Psy	Soc	Nurs	Me	Ma	Pa	Ps	Ed	Co	Man
Political Concepts: Power Force Authority Order Law											

Adapted from Lawton (1983)

For our 3-year basic nursing course, such meticulous process of matching will require several matrices with the possibility of sub-dividing some of the matrices. In each of the frames it should bepossible to identify subject-teachers or departments who can handle the new concepts, for example, "Law" (Table 12), and to identify and fill further gaps. This process will enable the modification and adaptation of existing courses and syllabuses to meet the new requirements of students in relation to the common curriculum and community-oriented education for health professionals.

Summary

This chapter has considered the issue of redesigning or revising an existing curriculum, or planning a new curriculum from the perspective of a health professional community-oriented educational institution. This exercise should be conducted at school, departmental and community levels and must involve all teachers and others concerned. Although time-consuming, the technique of comparing existing subjects with what is required in terms of the eight systems and curriculum-matrix analysis can be useful ways of detecting gaps and mismatches in a curriculum. The following chapter deals with the task of organizing the content produced by using these curriculum planning techniques.

9

Planning for a Community-Oriented Common Curriculum: Curriculum Organisation

This chapter considers issues concerning how to organise the common curriculum on the basis of cultural analysis conducted in the previous stages taking into consideration important educational strategies and procedures and psychological theories and questions that have a bearing on teaching and learning. The chapter begins with a look at the common curriculum idea as it applies to cultural analysis.

The Common curriculum idea

In the context of cultural analysis it is important for course planners to be clear about the meaning of common curriculum. A common curriculum should not be confused with the policy of having a uniform curriculum. It would be impossible, even if desirable to expect that all students learn the same amount of content from any teaching programme. This is not what should be intended in any case. The common curriculum idea demands that planners decide on the concepts and experiences which will give access to worthwhile knowledge and make it possible for all students to access this minimum programme. Some students will certainly progress much further, while some will fall behind in the basic understanding of the common curriculum programme. However, all students will have been given access to useful knowledge (Lawton 1983). Furthermore, in the context of cultural analysis, this common curriculum idea incorporates opportunities for curriculum planners to apply the principles of the curriculum process, community-based education, integrated learning, problem-based learning and other relevant educational theories, principles and approaches to guide the organization of the common curriculum and to increase skills in teamwork and bring about positive change in the attitudes of students toward various disciplines and peoples. It is important for curriculum planners to realize that as students cannot learn everything in a common curriculum they must include in their planning opportunities for students to develop ability to search for information, and to develop in knowledge and engage in life-long learning.

Without doubt, most course planners will agree on this point for, apart from its practical justification, it agrees very well with the educational principles we highlighted in previous chapters. Be it as it may, it will still be necessary for those planning the education of health professionals to work out the common curriculum approach that would best suit their individual situations, as long as the approach does not neglect any of the eight systems discussed in the previous chapters. As the Network of Community -Oriented Institutions for the Health Sciences (Schmidt et al 1991) suggests community-oriented programmes differ from country to country, and therefore a training institution in a developing country, for example, should not have the same curriculum as a training institution in a developed country when these countries do not have all health problems in common. This is why the cultural analysis approach requires that selection from the eight aspects of culture (Chapter 6) should be done with respect to a particular country or society.

The other point that should be made is that the idea of the common curriculum does not involve central direction of the curriculum (Lawton 1983). This issue is vital to the application of the cultural analysis approach to curriculum planning in the complex field of community health care and will be treated in detail in Chapter 10 on managing the curriculum innovation and change.

An effort to solve the problem of objectives came as a proposal that each aspect of the curriculum should be examined separately on the premise that various curricula activities or subject areas will need different curriculum planning approaches. (Stenhouse1975). As a result of this, certain writers have proposed a different type of separation of curriculum activities that can be justified educationally from those that are instrumental, kinds of training for which statements of intent are not only acceptable but even necessary. This eclectic approach is a proper and acceptable approach to planning a cultural analysis-type curriculum for health professional education and training for PHC/community health. The following sections discuss how curriculum planners can organize the common curriculum using these curriculum approaches, together with educational and psychological theories, principles and strategies in their planning.

Classification of Professional Knowledge

As already mentioned, in the curriculum planning process planners should consider the possibility of using curriculum models based on subjects or disciplines for two main reasons: maintaining the self –confidence of subject-specialist teachers and the need for schools to be concerned with public or professional knowledge, which is usually organized in subjects or disciplines.

Eraut (1994) has identified and classified three kinds of knowledge that underpin professional education, which Boaden et al (1999) discuss using examples of teaching methods in the community drawn from the literature. The first type of professional knowledge is Propositional Knowledge. It is connected to the discipline-based concepts, principles and generalizations that define general practice and that can be used in professional activities. The nature of propositional knowledge associated with community-based education refers to the content of the discipline such as epidemiology, statistics, decision-making, healthcare economics, ethics, computer science etc., all of which have been specified in the previous chapter on curriculum coverage. These elements are additional to the basic "core" of, for example, medicine (anatomy, biochemistry, physiology, etc) and are necessary for the effective practice of the discipline in the broader community -oriented health service. Such a "core" curriculum consists of a group of essential courses embodying the fundamental basis of medicine generally, or specifically, of community-oriented health care, and it is given to students before more individualized opportunities for focused study are presented. These components feed into the major areas of community-health practice such as disease prevention, environmental health and health care organization components which conventionally contained them. Therefore, the use of subjects in planning such a curriculum may be justifiable and necessary for including critical content in the curriculum concerning the eight elements of PHC/community health.

While the important link between propositional knowledge and community-based education cannot be denied, it is the manner in which students learn such core knowledge that has to change if it is tobe of much use.

Curriculum planners must consider ways by which students can use propositional knowledge through the higher order thinking skills of replication (the process of repeating what has been learnt), application (using knowledge in new situations), interpretation (bringing out the meaning of instructions and problems) and association (the process by which an association between a behaviour and a stimulus is learned; the assumption that ideas and experiences reinforce one another and can be linked to enhance the learning process), instead of the usual lower order thinking skill of recall that results from rote learning. They can achieve this learning through modes such as attachments to community institutions and resources, observing doctors and members of the health team, and data collection and dissemination (reports, etc). Classroom-based methods such as lectures and observation of experts can also aid the teaching-learning process.

Eraut's second type of professional knowledge is Personal knowledge and the interpretation of experience. This category refers to knowledge that the student gains passively from experiences that are not openly related to learning, particularly in situations where the concentration is to try and do things. Such learning experiences must be planned so that teachers and students can employ teaching and learning strategies and resources that shift the responsibility of searching and using information to the learner. For example, such learning steps can begin with motivating students to analyze their life-experiences, followed by arrangements that provide students the chance for discovery and reflection, and later, introducing students to theories and to abstract and general ideas. Eventually, students are provided opportunities to develop skills in developing plans, action planning and implementation of plans. Course planners must work out or adapt the teaching/learning strategies and resources that will suit such student-oriented learning processes, such as one-to-one teaching in the community that includes problem-solving, self-assessment and similar teaching and learning strategies.

Erauts's third category of professional knowledge is Process knowledge, which makes great use of propositional (or content) knowledge and is, according to Eraut, at the centre of professional practice. Process knowledge refers to knowing how to do things. Here, the student acquires and orders information, develops skilled behaviour (complex sequence of routinized actions), uses deliberative processes (e.g., planning, evaluating, analyzing and decision-making) gives information (e.g., communicates appropriately) and monitors himself (audit on activities in his practice). As has been mentioned earlier, there is increasing need to strengthen and expand the preparation of health professionals for roles in PHC/Community Health, as evidence from the relevant literature indicates. For example, a global study (Hirschfeld et al 1997) to examine the strengthening of nursing and midwifery services showed that globally there is agreement that nurses and midwives should obtain more education than is now available. In addition, the study identified not only needs for better preparation in PHC, but also needs for more skills in PHC in the community and in nurse clinics, and in work in different sectors of health care systems. Despite the problems the objectives approach to curriculum planning pose, the approach as already mentioned, can be valuable especially where some kind of clear goals as a prerequisite for being a rational activity is required, such as in planning the teaching of important tasks in clinical settings where, for example, patients from PHC villages are referred. In such community clinical settings, the students should be assisted to acquire basic skills (acceptable "core"), which, as we mentioned before, translates to a level of achievement, their understanding and ability in crucial areas of knowledge and skills that the student can use in adult and working-life. These skills should be "broad-based and transferable, rather specific and job-restricted, and should include that range known as social and life skills, as exemplified in Chapter 6 on curriculum coverage. Needless to say, the principles, approaches and procedures that can, for example, make learning effective by making such learning relevant, which we have highlighted in previous discussion, must guide such education.

Multiple Curricular Approaches

To facilitate students' use of professional knowledge through replication, application, interpretation and association, guided by the principles of the curriculum process (and cooperative learning), curriculum planners can employ curriculum process, integrated curriculum, and problem-based and community-based approaches to learning in their planning. These approaches can be considered closely linked concepts in community health practice and are discussed here together.

In Chapter 3 we presented strong justification for selecting the process curriculum model as a principal model for planning a cultural-analysis type curriculum for health professional education for PHC/community health. Let us now look at the tasks which face the curriculum planner who seeks to incorporate such a model in the curriculum. The planner should re-structure subject matter, such as the subject matter identified in the previous chapter on curriculum coverage in Chapter 7 to make clear basic structure, making sure that knowledge which produces further knowledge is better than knowledge that does not. The aim is not only specification and transmission of a body of knowledge but the encouragement and guidance of a process of discovery undertaken by the students that is based on the principles of the curriculum process model outlined in Chapter 3. He/she must look at the methods used by the intellectual practitioner in community health for the processes they use in their work, such as Eraut's identification and classification of professional knowledge described above, and adopt these processes in his teaching plans. Such practitioners are the PHC/community health experts, educators, epidemiologists, social scientists, etc. He should use the evidence obtained from a detailed study of people living in the community in re-structuring the curriculum.

Additionally, the planning must include deliberate efforts to provide opportunities for students to learn how to cross-apply the processes they have mastered. In other words the ways and means of putting them in good use in various settings in PHC/community health. The accomplishment of these tasks, together with attending to many of the issues raised in Chapter 7 and the final chapter on managing the curriculum innovation and change (Chapter 10) will lead to a productive cultural analysis common curriculum design.

One issue that planners need to consider with respect to the use of these approaches to student learning in the community has been mentioned above briefly: possible loss of the subject specialization of some teachers, with the possible consequent loss of their identity and security that relating to a specific subject provides. But this is perhaps greater than the advantages of integration if the curriculum is totally integrated, which may not necessarily be the case here. Furthermore, one must consider the positive result from most kinds of integrated curricula- the positive effects in the altered relationships between teachers, and, especially, between teachers and students. Indeed, the rationale for integration, which consists of reorganization of content of the curriculum in accordance with some cross -disciplinary theme, and which frequently leads to alterations in content itself, and addition and reduction of new ideas, thereby motivating positive discussion among teachers and for curriculum revision, must be given more recognition by curriculum planners. But efforts aimed at introduction of a totally integrated curriculum, completely setting aside subjects, advises caution here. Each form of integration will present its own problems and, therefore, each should be considered on its own importance.

However, in order to better incorporate the elements of PHC/community health, there is now much stress on the need for the kind of reorganization and regrouping of subjects that the integrated curriculum (of which the "core" curriculum is considered to be a variation) framework can provide. This development is a response to pressure to restructure knowledge to meet changing social needs. Such pressures, as we have seen, include views about education such as those that see education as being fundamentally concerned with developing the experience of the individual. In other words, the student must be put in a situation in which he can organize his knowledge in ways that are meaningful to him as well as to society. The educational benefits that can result from integrating the education of health professionals with such health and social systems are indeed significant. Clinics and health centres in which doctors, nurses, midwives, students, etc., collaborate can, for example, help to co-ordinate activities between biomedical and ethno-medical practitioners who provide basic health services in many villages and form the nucleus of primary health workers in the majority of our local populations. Such integrated clinics which can become centres for research on medical plants, for instance, should provide a culturally holistic approach to illness and student learning in various aspects of primary health care and community health including appropriate technology, traditional medicine, etc.

Indeed, perhaps the most important influence on the curriculum in recent years has been the pressure to development PHC as an integrated health system, as evidenced by several WHO proposals (e.g. WHO 1996). The benefits of this approach are expressed in terms of several outcomes and gains: improved efficiency and productivity, improved health status, improved user satisfaction, and convenience and improved equity and accountability. For example, the integration of family planning with education, health and welfare programmes provides important lateral support for family planning. This effort is part of a larger strategy to have fertility control become not only accepted in principle but made real in practice.

Interestingly, examples of this type of regrouping and reorganization to meet the requirements of integrated studies are that which are taking place at institutions like the Gambia College School of Nursing and Midwifery. Here, the Basic Nurse Curriculum has been changed from a subject-centered curriculum to an integrated-curriculum, using the "Activities of Living" nursing model, which incorporates the "Nursing Process" [a problem-solving approach], as an integrative framework, with emphasis on important areas like PHC/Community health.

Whatever the curriculum integration employed, course planners must consider two aspects of integration that can be helpful in planning common curriculum structures (Greeves 1984). One aspect is content integration which relates to the relationships among the knowledge, skills and values learned. The other component is the mechanical structure of integration, in which the ideas of continuity, sequence and integration are emphasized. Here, there is vertical reiteration of content elements (continuity). Previous experience is built on, with concepts and ideas being broadened and deepened (sequence), and there is horizontal relationship of the knowledge, skills and values to be learned (integration). As suggested earlier, this calls for departmental planning where groups of teachers can formulate a common curriculum for the whole school. This kind of detailed planning is best done in departments by teaching groups (and other collaborators) and should involve syllabus construction.

However, the main focus of the planning of integration should be on integrated learning. This, as opposed to integrated teaching, which is teacher-oriented, a basic shortcoming in student learning, is a learner-oriented programme with built-in-relevance and supported by the gaining of problem-solving skills which consists of educational activities designed to help the student and lead him to achieve the needed integration by his own efforts (Guilbert 1987).

Organizational problems usually raised by not only interdisciplinary education, integrated studies, problem-based and community-based learning, and other education approaches and the need for arrangements that will help overcome such problems should be given due attention by the curriculum planners. Many of the institutions engaged in such education implemented new educational approaches without much attention to the possible need for modification of existing management strategies. In other instances, alternative semi-autonomous organizational arrangements were set up by the established schools. Many educational institutions for health professionals have undoubtedly tried to improve this situation by adopting existing relevant organizational arrangements or devising new ones, on the basis of the differing ideas on education as we observed earlier. The result has still been a proliferation of many different and sometimes conflicting managerial arrangements in educational institutions and clinical settings (Kahssay 1998). With regard to interdisciplinary education, for example, there are numerous efforts to accomplish more effective interdisciplinary programmes providing experiences relevant to work in a health team. Thus model health centres for the delivery of health care have been established and are used for training different categories of health personnel simultaneously. In other programmes, courses have been developed to be taken by students of different health professions, or programmes have selected core or common –entry curricula across disciplines. Other programmes have attempted to create organizational structures conducive to co-operation. Some have added courses that make application of theory and discussion of patient care in a multi-disciplinary setting possible. Still other programmes have stressed community-based learning and problem-based learning (Stephenson et al 2002). Apart from the differing approaches to such education, health centres where interdisciplinary education is provided have been generally sidelined by vertical programmes despite their critical position of delivering and linking a variety of services for the benefit of people's health. Despite the Alma-Ata Declaration, and even sometimes in opposition to it, vertical programmes have continued, and indeed flourished.

Paradoxically, the most debilitating aspect of these programmes for health development is that they are solution-based. They emphasize targets to be reached instead of building up systems that have the capacity to promote health and solve health problems. All these add to the factors outlined in Chapter 7 that diminish community of learning in community health. In these contexts, there are organizational challenges that are suggestive of common problems experienced by teachers who operate in educational programmes in which interdisciplinary education approaches are used, or problems anticipated by teachers who plan to teach in such programmes: on-going financial commitment, time demanding on clinicians and community resources who are committed to an interdisciplinary approach in curriculum planning, keeping curriculum content on an interdisciplinary theme without a heavy focus on medicine, for example, and identifying an appropriate evaluation tool to measure effectiveness and impact of an interdisciplinary experience. There can be useful ways to tackle such problems in interdisciplinary education. In the first instance, the curriculum which should aim at developing the individual must be an issue of negotiation between the various participants (including the student himself or herself), that employs two mechanisms: personal programme and the use of contracts. The personal programme is the outcome of the student's efforts at selecting with the guidance of his or her tutor areas he or she needs to learn and how to go about doing so, and the vocational orientation of such learning. The use of contracts is realized between the various agencies contributing to the different learning experiences in a programme [like members of the multidisciplinary health team] and the professional educational institutions concerned. Counselling and guidance and assessment are another important and necessary requirement for achieving the aim of such preparation. Planners can consider using the student profile as part of the guidance that is provided to all students as it should be a proper method for meeting the learner's needs. The student profile presents to planners a common system of record-keeping and certification, making redundant the need for an overall pass/fail grade. It allows the recognition of important personal qualities which cannot be formally assessed. This method of recording assessment has been shown to be a progressive way of combining counselling, guidance and assessment and making them a single aspect of closely interconnecting elements.

Thus, it is crucial that planners pay particularly attention to creating the right kind of placement support systems for students and staff in the community, such as supervisors and mentors. This is because in community placements media resources, for example, are limited than in hospital environments and therefore, for example, the mentor relies much more on role modelling and discussion strategies. A supervisor can be considered to be an appropriately qualified experienced senior health professional that has been prepared for making sure that relevant experience is given to students to equip them with worthwhile knowledge and skills and to facilitate the student's progress in his or her learning by overseeing such learning. A mentor can also be seen to be an appropriately qualified experienced senior health professional who has been prepared in much the same way as a supervisor, but who by facilitation and example guides, assists and supports students in learning new skills, behaviour and attitudes. It is widely agreed that personal characteristics, clinical expertise, motivation and teaching skills are crucial in selecting such staff for their roles in the community. Chapter 10 on managing the innovation and change includes discussion on approaches to preparing teachers for their roles. A problem often expressed particularly among students in regard to integrated, problem-based and community-based learning is that the environments for such learning do not always adequately provide the diversity, sequence and continuity in learning students require, especially if they are used permanently or most of the time for practical experiences. It seems that experimentation is a very useful means to solving such organizational problems in specific situations. However, there are approaches that may prove to be effective. For example, in order to enhance sequence and continuity in student learning in training centres and similar learning environments, learning experiences that centre on, for example, community diagnosis can be arranged so that a group of students that had already been introduced to community diagnosis is able to build on (e.g., at the project implementation stage) a previous group's work in the process, like data analysis, instead of repeating the community diagnosis process. Another problem that requires the attention of curriculum planners arises from the need to provide greater opportunities to students going through these types of learning for more freedom of movement and greater application of discovery learning strategies and other strategies that such learning requires.

In constructing such detailed programmes, course planners must necessarily use logical, psychological, social and scientific principles (e.g., Bruner (1960), Thorndike (1931) and Gagne (1985) that can help produce the best patterns of sequencing and ordering. Although in medicine, for example, the pattern of ordering may be clearly visible, questions concerning "when" and "how long" components of learning, should be the focus of professional course planners. Therefore, principles of timing and length of units and lessons, and principles guiding the presentation of information and learning experiences are crucial. Also important are principles of logic that, for example, relate to pre-requisite knowledge, and the progression from such knowledge, from the particular to the general, and from the theoretical to the concrete, and the kind of content and the students' familiarity with it. Questions of 'readiness' (a law which states that learning is dependent upon the learner's eagerness to learn) and the idea of the 'spiral curriculum' (in which students repeat the study of a subject at various grade levels, each time at a higher level of difficulty and in greater depth) are also worth considering. Curriculum planners should also try in their planning to meet the requirement to provide various strategies, approach, procedures, resources, etc, that will suit different kinds of learners and their learning styles.

Of particular importance also are the concepts and principles of primary health care and community health (Chapter 1). These principles are creating opportunities in some countries that have stimulated a series of new ideas and paradigms in, among other things, the ordering and sequencing of integrated curricula and other types of curricula. There are numerous descriptions of educational programmes that require, for example, immediate and continuous involvement of students in PHC/community health field work. Thus, a planning that departments must attend to is changing from a teacher-oriented to a student-oriented process. The principles of self-reliance, equity, community participation and inter-sectoral collaboration, which are the cornerstones of PHC/community health, demand that the role of the student should change from being one of a passive learner to that of an active one. Therefore, experiential learning which changes the traditional relationship between teacher and student according to the new realities must be emphasized. Such a change must place students in settings that resemble the settings of their future work or which motivate problem analysis (as already outlined above). The aim of such planning, therefore, is to link methods, strategies and approaches to learning closely with the community environment and characteristics of what needs to be learnt. Boaden et al (1999) describe a useful model (Figure 5) of four educational stages for learning clinical skills in the community that demonstrates how such linkages can be achieved in the planning of student learning in the community through the use of logical, psychological, social and scientific principles and the concepts and principles of PHC. In the first stage, exploration, the medical student, for example, starts community experience as a setting for clinical work. For instance, the student gets used to the new environment, observes and follows a senior doctor and mentor; he conducts some interviews, and uses some diagnostic tools. The student then progresses to the second and third educational stages in the development of clinical learning of skills in the community-skill development and increasing independence in learning, respectively. At the second stage the student is, for example, exposed more widely to the community and the practice environment; he or she takes more history and engages in clinical procedures under supervision, and discusses management plans. At stage three the student, for example, performs clinical skills in a more reasonable period with minimal supervision, improves presentations and case writing skills, draws up a differential diagnosis, takes part in clinical audit, and is increasingly aware of community networks. At the fourth stage of development of clinical learning-co-operative learning- the medical student is capable of carrying out certain critical actions such as unsupervised practice, using effective communications skills, learning with others, using community and referral procedures appropriately, and involving members of the team appropriately.

Figure 5: Phases of learning in the Community

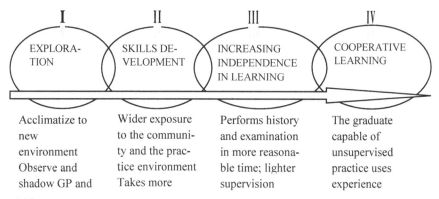

I	II	III	IV
EXPLORA-TION	SKILLS DE-VELOPMENT	INCREASING INDEPENDENCE IN LEARNING	COOPERATIVE LEARNING
Acclimatize to new environment Observe and shadow GP and	Wider exposure to the community and the practice environment Takes more	Performs history and examination in more reasonable time; lighter supervision	The graduate capable of unsupervised practice uses experience

team members
Use some diag-
nostic tools e.g.,
BP, eyes and ears
Observe consulta-
tions and
become aware of
patient
centered approach
Carry out some
interviews
Become aware of
the
discipline of clini-
cal practice,
of doctor, patient
relationships
and team- work

focused history
and carries out
physical
examinations
under
supervision
Practice case
presentation
and note -writing
Uses basic and
clinical science to
explain clinical
and psychosocial
features
Can discuss rudi-
mentary
management
plans Competent
in emergency
procedures

Improves presen-
tation and
case writing
skills
Can plan & evalu-
ate initial
management for
range of common
conditions
Can draw up a
differential
diagnosis
Can plan some
investigations
and perform some
Learns to become
a member of a
team
Builds up a case
load Takes part in
clinical audits
Increasingly
aware of
community net-
works

as the basis for
learning
Incorporates
psychological
and social ele-
ment s in
management
plans
Involves team
members
appropriately
Uses effective
communication
skills both in
consultations and
in practice
Able to continue
learning in asso-
ciation with oth-
ers
Sensitive to re-
source issues in
clinical practice
Selective in use
of community
and referral

Boaden et al (1999)

Thus, utilization of the small-group in backgrounds like the clinics as a learn-ing setting is another planning that must be done by departments. There is no doubt as to the educational justification of this strategy. For one thing, students can be gently, but firmly, imbued with the attitude that it isdesirable and en-joyable to learn and work harmoniously in groups with other pupils. As a re-sult classes can be remarkably self-organizing, which makes teachers' work-loads far less onerous than they might otherwise be. Moreover, the small-group strategy has the advantage of creating possibilities for students to learn the values and skills of inter-working with other members of the multidisciplinary health team. As the analysis of the social system in Chapter 5 shows, quite often health professionals in many countries justify working alone in clinical settings on the basis of easeand speed. Furthermore, the interdisciplinary and interpersonal tension that may result from co-operating with others in a team is often a reason for lack of collaboration. In addition, the hierarchical relationships and specialization which traditional clinical care still fosters are important constraints to collaboration. For example, several barriers to team work and interdisciplinary education have been reported by Wolf (1999). She also presents predictors for teamwork and concern for patients including orientation toward group problem-solving confidence, and a positive self-efficacy toward group process. Although respect for colleagues exists among health care providers, this has been inadequate to avoid self-defeating rivalries that have constrained improvements in health professional education. Therefore, curriculum planners must try to overcome such organizational hurdles involved which are not without trouble.

Additionally, the focus of the planning should be to provide the learning opportunities that will develop knowledge, skills and understanding in mediation, advocacy and negotiation, and inculcate the values of tolerance that are needed to encourage inter-sectoral collaboration. Such learning experiences must be planned so that teachers and students can employ teaching and learning strategies and resources that shift the responsibility of searching and using information to the learner.

For example, teaching- learning steps can begin with motivating students to analyze their life-experiences, followed by arrangements that provide students the chance for discovery and reflection, and later, introducing students to theories and to abstract and general ideas. Eventually, students are provided opportunities to develop skills in developing plans, action planning and implementation of plans. Course planners must work out or adapt the teaching/learning strategies and resources that will suit such student-oriented learning processes. Planners must look for suitable arrangements for the new schemes such as workshops and relevant educational facilities. It will be necessary to, for instance, timetable together subjects to be integrated and deal with the fears that the new schemes will require less structure and more flexibility in the use of time, and resistance to such learning options. There may be demands for additional/or new materials and resources, and the planner must ensure these requirements are provided or produced by teachers where and when necessary. Storage and retrieval of such materials by teachers must also be considered by planners. Although adequate resources and materials may not always be a precondition for effective learning in the community there may be the need for resources, such as problem identification committees, where "paper cases" (standardized cases that may be formulated by faculty) are used, instead of real patients/clients in problem-based learning. However, the use of "paper cases" poses other problems, apart from the possible lack of them. The learning of problem-solving on the basis of problems derived directly from unreal patients or clients is inadequate or ineffective for preparing health professionals for problem-solving particularly in clinical or community practice. Because of this problems obtained from both "paper cases" and real patients should be used in PB programmes. This relates mainly to the need for health professionals to be able to integrate learning (vertical and horizontal). In addition, an approach that involves the teaching of basic health sciences well before students are in contact with patients on the clinical areas seriously limits the effectiveness of integration and problem-solving in such learning. To solve this problem, teachers should change to the use of methods that encourage students to learn the basic sciences on the basis of identified real patient's problems, not in isolation of such problems. Indeed, this is the method used at The Gambia College School of Nursing and Midwifery where, as was mentioned, the basic sciences are learned simultaneously in dealing with patient's problems, along with other content in an integrated manner, aided by the "Activities of Living" elements. This indeed proves extremely stimulating to students. However, problem-based learning has a tendency to produce anxiety in students due to the limitless knowledge that they need to acquire to deal with a problem and must therefore have to learn to set limits to such knowledge. Students must be helped to do this without anxiety in their problem-solving activities.

Approaches to Curriculum Evaluation

As outlined in Chapter 7, there are fairly seven kinds of evaluation which are required from time to time in most educational systems, such as estimates of pupil performance and or competence. However, for the purpose of showing how curriculum planners can address the question of accountability on the basis of cultural analysis we shall consider Lawton's (1983) six-fold analysis of evaluation models which are 'ideal types' rather than exemplars of actual practice. These are outlined as follows:

Model 1: Classical (or agricultural –botanical research) model: This model handles the issue of evaluating a curriculum project or a teaching style like that of a research experiment in agriculture or botany. This should show whether the programme in the experimental group is superior to that in the control group which had not been exposed to the new programme.

Model 2: Research and development (or industrial/factory) model: According to this model, all curriculum development should start with research, one result of which would be a clarification of aims. The industrialist must know exactly what he is trying to produce; the school must know what kind of disparity in pupil behaviour will be achieved.

Model 3: Illuminative (or anthropological) model: This model has been proposed only as a reaction against the Classical and Research and Development models, but was in a positive way an attempt towards anthropological methods of evaluation. The importance of this kind of evaluation in terms of cultural analysis is that it was a move away from myopic psychological views of teaching and learning and presents the classroom as part of an intricate cultural situation.

Model 4: Briefing decision-makers (or political) model: This model views evaluation as that which should not be directed towards providing information about the positive results of teaching or learning, but with information about which decisions to be made. It can consist of three ideal types of evaluation

(a) Bureaucratic evaluation: This is an open-door policy service to those government agencies controlling educational resources. The evaluator accepts the values of those holding office (the administrator) and supplies information to help them reach their policy objectives. His report is controlled by the bureaucrats, in return for pittance he gives information and advice and has no responsibility over absolute decision.

(b) Autocratic evaluation: This pattern/form of evaluation involves conditional service. The evaluator supplies external recommendations. Values are reached from the evaluator's perception of the constitutional and moral obligation of the technocrats. The focus is upon issues of educational merit, the role of the evaluator is the professional. The techniques of study must be seen as earning scientific proofs. The evaluator maintains ownership of his (her) report. The evaluator is the 'autocrat' in this model.

(c) Democratic evaluation: Here, an information service is provided to the whole community. Sponsorship by one group (for example, the administrators) does not give them claim to advice or secret information. The assumption behind this model is 'value pluralism' – there is no widely held concept about basic values. The only value which can be reached is the desirability of an informed citizenry. The job of the democratic evaluator is that of 'an honest broker'. The report must be written so that it is available to non-specialists. The evaluation report will be non- recommendatory.

Model 5: Teacher as researcher (the professional) model: This model proposes that the curriculum the teacher reaches at/develops will not be right or wrong, but will be assessed by whether it advances knowledge or not. It is a thrust through which to explore and test hypotheses, to a recommendation to be adopted. One of the stakes here is that of role conflict: The teacher has to be both someone who indicates learning, and also the participant- observer trying to assess success and failure in the classroom. The great advantage of this approach is that the values of the school and the culture of the classroom maintain their significance.

Model 6: Case study (or portrayal) model: This model stresses maintenance of, where appropriate, some of the traditional methods of measurement including surveys, checklists and questionnaires. Such approaches may also rely on other more impressionistic methods forming a basis for their whole study. This eclectic approach is sometimes referred to as case study which connotes a modified version of illuminative evaluation According to Lawton, cultural analysis is more at par with evaluation models 3-6 in contrast to models 1 & 2. Lawton argues that the claim advanced by many administrators that the cultural analysis methods might be said to be strong on justification, but apparently weak on evaluation is not necessarily the case. Cultural analysis methods can and should be applied at every stage of the model and at every level of evaluation. For example, with regard to Evaluation Type 1: Estimates of pupil progress or competence, in devising a test or other assessment instrument, the teacher must ask certain prior questions:

(a) How worthwhile this learning really is? (if not, do not test it – drop it).

(b) How important is the learning intrinsically (i.e., in its own right).

(c) How important is it chronologically (i.e., how essential is it in the wider context of past and future learning?

(d) What are the most vital characteristics of what has been learned (for example, memorization of facts compared with understanding concepts of generalizations?)

(e) How can I best develop/create and effect assessment instruments (i.e. effective in terms of response to pupils, and a basis for future learning)?

(f) How can I change/reverse assessment into a useful record of progress?

In this way, class evaluation becomes not an afterthought to the teaching process, but an important part of the planning and record keeping.

This approach creates possibilities for curriculum planners to consider the kinds of formative or alternative evaluations that are not only based on summative evaluation or examinations. While the differences between formative and summative assessment may sometimes be unclear, here formative assessment is regarded as the alternative evaluation or general observations and judgments that are made and summative assessment as examinations, which aim to assist in grouping students within a subject, to help in end of year reports, planning of student's programmes and to help in determining qualifications for employment. For example, the evaluation concerns of a professional training institution may identify categories of measures for evaluation purposes such as entry measures, study progress measures, institutional descriptions, unobtrusive measures, course descriptions, exit measures, career reviews and practice surveys.

On the basis of the evaluation criteria of relevance, reliability, rater error, objectivity, predictability and accountability, alternative evaluation methods such as the unobtrusive measures have been critically analyzed with positive results in health professional education, for example, nursing education (e.g., Gorham 1963). Checklists and rating scales have been found to be more ideal where effort was minimal, because they are easier to fill out and their format more familiar to most nurses.

Observational forms have proved to be more accurate, and also more suitable for research projects, since investigators can modify and develop the forms or structure new ones. Items on evaluation

forms could be rated in a consistent way, and total scores could provide evidence of valid indicators of equality of performance. Students who are taught by formative evaluation without grades have been found to have learned significantly more than those who learned by other means with grades.

Moreover, the value of this form of assessment in nursing education is shown by experiences of student self-evaluation: the trusting and cooperative quality to student-teacher relationship; the writing of anecdotes by students which offers potential for growth in critical thinking, and as a result of self-evaluative experiences, students became more perceptive in recognizing and responding to patient needs. In addition, other modes of assessment of students' performance are highly illustrative of the value of alternative methods. The disguised measure, for instance, has the advantage of increased likelihood of obtaining a valid assessment of the beliefs and value of students. The simulation method is likewise advantageous because it ensures that all students face the same clinical problems or content. Indeed, another alternative mode of assessment which was also mentioned above-the use of student profiles in the assessment of students' progress in their education – rests on similar strategies and techniques. Here again, student profiles can serve as a substitute for grading.

Student profiles, as we noted earlier, are a kind of evidence of the student's capabilities in educational (and non-educational) aspects. Profiles give all the important features of a student. In Chapter 3 we briefly looked at assessment in terms of the process model, which although pointing to difficulties for the assessment of student work provides, inter-alia, wider scope for teacher development. This assessment may not be totally subjective as it attracts public criteria. And in its logically pure form the process model implies that in assessment or appraisal the teacher ought to be a critic, not a marker. Indeed, the requirement to assess worthwhile activities demands such an approach to assessment. But despite all their usefulness, however, such alternative modes of assessment have some problems of validity, which need to be looked at. This is important mainly because these alternative modes of evaluation are increasingly providing, or are increasingly being considered important frameworks for making judgments about community-oriented educational programmes, despite the apparent "obsession" with objectives.

Recognition of the wider implications of educational evaluation should lead to the possibilities of originating participatory evaluation programme processes. Tenn et al (1994) case study description of a participatory process of curriculum development based on primary health care includes an outline of an evaluation programme process. At this important point of the process of curriculum development, endorsement of the process and examination of data results was conducted by means of a reformed advisory committee made up mainly by nurse representatives. Participation of different stakeholders was requested for the evaluation process.

The evaluation advisory committee took responsibilities that comprised deciding on the mandate, specifying the degree of the evaluation process, the membership of those serving in the committee, the topics to be discussed and the use of the results. Instead of inviting all relevant users of information, stakeholders and decision-makers to be members of the evaluation advisory committee, an evaluation plan that would favour the participation of different individuals, groups and agencies at various points in the evaluation process was used.

The Patton (1986) evaluation plan was chosen mainly due to not only the implicit roles of the different stakeholders, users of information and decision-makers, but also because of other rules, such as the good chance of interpretation of the theoretical ideas into actions that the majority of people were familiar with, the incorporation of both short-term and long-term analysis of findings and outcomes, and the different evaluation devices used. Patton (1978) advises programme evaluators and researchers to depart from the natural science paradigm of hypothetico-deductive methodology, with its concentration on experimental design, quantitative measurement, and multivariate, parametric statistical analysis. He suggests a substitute, contingent on anthropological methods, which emphasizes detailed description and qualitative notes, in-depth interviewing and participant- observation. According to Tenn et al, ratification with others seemingly established the suitability of the inclusive evaluation model to the social and cultural actualities, the inadequate statistical means available to the project and the ideology of participation.

We shall have to return to the crucial issue of evaluation in the next and final chapter, where it will be clear that not only is evaluation frequently misused, but proposals like empowerment of communities by involving them in the planning of education for health manpower, including curriculum evaluation, are also often subject to political constraints that emanate from within as well as from outside health educational institutions.

Summary

In summary, this chapter has looked at how to organise the common curriculum on the basis of cultural analysis conducted in the previous stages. This eclectic approach proposed is a proper and acceptable approach to planning a cultural analysis- type common curriculum for health professional education and training for PHC/community health. In this planning process curriculum planners should consider the possibility of using different kinds of curriculum models, such as those based on subjects or disciplines, the integrated and process curriculum models. They must consider ways by which students can use knowledge appropriately in their learning in the community. To do so they must try in their planning to meet the requirements to provide various strategies, approaches, procedures, resources, etc., that will suit not only different kinds of learners and their learning styles, but also the needs of community – based education. Approaches such as the student-centered approach to teaching and learning are particularly crucial. The use of logical, psychological, social and scientific principles that have a bearing on teaching and learning in addition to the principles and concepts of PHC and community health can help planners produce the best kind of curricula based on the cultural analysis framework. Community-oriented educational programmes are able to accommodate the realities of health care through integration of health professional training into the systems in which they function; emphasis should be placed by instructors on the PHC principles of community participation, inter-sectoral collaboration, equity and self-reliance. Student learning must focus on implementing action-oriented plans, and such learning should be incremental, from the simple to the complex, and from what is familiar to what is new. Additionally, role modelling should be used to bring about needed changes in rewards. How the leader and his or her team of planners can deal with the organizational issues raised by the use of the many educational approaches will be the subject of the last chapter on managing the innovation and change.

10

Managing the Curriculum Innovation and Change

In Chapter 7 we saw that the factors which influence curriculum planning are not confined to institutions only, they also come from outside the boundaries of educational institutions, posing critical challenges to the innovator and his or her faculty team. The numerous difficulties and pressures which make up the social and political contexts in which curriculum planning takes place and which, therefore, will influence the character and trend of curriculum planning were looked at. Chapter 8 looked at how to cover the content of the common curriculum adequately. Chapter 9 considered how curriculum planners can organize the common curriculum based on the Cultural Analysis approach. How can all these requirements for curriculum planning based on the cultural analysis approach, most of which will be new to teachers be fitted in health professional educational institutions? How can the curriculum be changed effectively to a PHC/ Community health and cultural analysis-type common curriculum, considering all the many issues that influence organizational innovation and change? Several issues are raised by the above questions which a team leader who seeks to effect innovation and change in educational institutions must address. To do so, he or she must reckon with many people and agencies in curriculum planning and curriculum innovation and change. Innovation is precisely the bringing in of something new to a particular establishment. This includes procedures already created nationally but new to a specific institution. Curriculum innovation has been categorized on a number of dimensions of change (Hoyle 1972): The rate of change may be rapid or slow; the scale may be large or small; the degree fundamental or superficial; the continuity revolutionary or evolutionary; and the direction linear or cyclical. Although innovation means a new idea, it is also a process in which ideas are to be adopted. Whereas innovation is the creation of something new, adaptation entails accepting an innovation that was planned by someone or a body outside a particular establishment.

We shall now consider how to manage the curriculum innovation and change with particular reference to the will or purposes of teachers and their collaborators in curriculum planning. In doingso, several of the conceptual and operative constraints of curriculum planning and the implementation of curriculum innovation and change will be discussed. In looking at the factors which influence curriculum planning in Chapter 7, we began with the community as a powerful context for learning. Here, we must also necessarily start with the community with a view to demonstrating how the innovator and his or her team can establish and build community of learning in community - oriented education for health professionals.

Building a Community of Learning

In chapter 7 we mentioned that despite community being so crucial for student learning in higher education, today learning in community has diminished due to several factors. These include expansion of large public institutions to accommodate government-mandated support of larger enrolments, leading to the emphasis of efficiency in structuring processes and to larger class sizes; increasing demands on faculty for research productivity outside the classroom; increasing numbers of commuter students, and an increasingly secularized society. The innovator and his team can rebuild community thereby strengthening learning. Bickford et al (2010) describe three ways through which this can be done: learning space design, information technology, community and information exchange, and pedagogical, curricular, and co-curricular design for learning. The innovator and his or her team need to explore how building community helps the creation of spaces for learning (and conversely, how creating learning-centered spaces can enhance our ability to build community); how technology can foster community and information exchange; and how community in curricular, co-curricular and pedagogical design fosters learning.

1. Learning Space Design

- This is about designing new learning places that encourage communication rather than distance.
- It includes a community of facilities managers, faculty, student development professionals, administrators, architects, students, technologists and other stakeholders.
- It involves a process of discussion and innovation to create spaces that will re-engage students and staff in the teaching and learning process.
- This multiple view is required by the complex students' projects to give the needed information for making informed decisions in team learning.

Bickford et al offer five steps to harness the full potential of community and to engage community in co-creating the built learning environment:

(1) Inviting stakeholders to contribute

- Invite people with various views to participate in decision-making on learning space design.

(2) Selecting and empowering a gifted leader

- Select a leader who can build community as well as create settings safe for participation and team learning.
- He or she should have vision, empathy and should be able to listen and value various perspectives.
- He or she must be empowered to carry out the needed tasks.
- He or she should be able to empower others.

(3) Understanding and respecting different views

- This includes inviting students and faculty input on learning space design.
- It includes encouraging participation of individuals and understanding of differences in views, culture, power and hierarchy and urging sensitiveness to those dissimilarities.

(4) Eradicating barriers to community learning

- This includes preventing obstruction of collaboration in community learning by various communication styles and values of actors in the education process.
- It includes dealing with differences in knowledge and expertise, personality differences and group dynamics.
- It includes dealing with barriers that come from processes and systems that can prevent consensus formation (for example, determining who should fund the building of an integrated living-learning

centre, academics or residential areas) (Bickford et al 2010).

(5) Balancing performance and patience

- This involves exercising patience to encourage new ideas to grow.

- However, endless discussion and debate should not be allowed as it can be time-consuming and costly.

- Past accomplishments should be considered when designing new learning space models to avoid costly mistakes.

2. Technology, Community, and Information Exchange

- This involves delivering academic programmes or conducting face-to-face

- classes in various physical spaces using technology in or out of the space.

- In these learning situations technology should be used to foster learning

- through building community as well as creating and sharing knowledge within the group, while allowing interaction to take place in and outside the formal classroom setting.

- ICTs can foster community by making communication outside the classroom richer and more extensive, and classroom time free for more active learning approaches.

- Using ICTs students can research or write papers while networking to build community.

- Communication tools such as enterprise-level e-mail and calendaring as well as learning management systems are important tools for learning and information exchange.

- However, there is a surprising lag in the widespread development and adoption of applications that allow the spontaneous and ad-hoc teaming, which characterizes an active community.

- The planning of physical space must consider the fact that face-to-face classroom meetings will become less didactic and more active, which encourages student participation and engagement in original learning approaches.

3. Pedagogical, Curricular, and Co-curricular Design

- This involves students engaging in many activities to form the social interactions needed to establish and build community.

- Students can achieve this without important faculty involvement, or faculty can shape, contribute to, and extend the learning environment of students.

- Professional development opportunities provide faculty the chance to experience student life again, which makes them value the possibilities of a learning community.
- Learning communities are increasingly common in faculty development programmes, where they provide a valuable learning process for those engaged in knowledge generation/production.
- Learning communities encourage open discussion and sharing among faculty and other stakeholders in the educational process.
- Learning communities assist participants deal with questions that relate to the nature of students and how they can be helped to learn.
- Learning and teaching centres in higher education provide strong mechanisms for stimulating institutional change that encompasses pedagogical, curricular, and co-curricular approaches which include faculty learning communities, experimental classrooms, support of student learning, and evaluation of student learning.
- Teaching and learning centres advance partnerships between student development and faculty by, for instance, preparing faculty to facilitate learning in community, where they can serve as valuable change agents for the curricular, pedagogical and co-curricular innovations that advance community.

Thus, according to Bickford et al, building a community of learning can be achieved through three forms of strategic instruments that can advance learning through the community processes of designing spaces that support learning, using information and communication technologies, and designing structures for learning that include pedagogy, curricular and co-curricular programming. They are: (1) learning space design, which involves inviting people with various perspectives in participatory decision-making, selecting and empowering a talented leader who is able to tap into the potential of community, understanding and appreciating differences in perspective in decision-making, eliminating roadblocks to community learning, and balancing patience and performance; (2) technology, community, and information exchange, with particular reference to the role of communication in building a community of learning, and use of information and communication technologies in building a community of learning and; (3) pedagogical, curricular, and co-curricular design, focusing on faculty planned pedagogical, curricular, and co-curricular activities, students' creation of learning activities that foster a community of learning, professional development opportunities that strengthen a community of learning, and the role of learning and teaching centres in building a community of learning.

Six Good Practices in Design Processes of Development Interventions
Complementing and supporting the above plan are six good practices in any design process of a development intervention (IFAD 2011):

- Involving stakeholders who can usefully participate in the design.
- Conducting a comprehensive situational analysis with primary stakeholders to have a better knowledge of the context as a basis for designing the relevant building strategy and implementation and evaluation processes.
- Creating a logical and achievable building strategy that clearly indicates the goal and objectives that will be achieved together with the anticipated outputs and activities.
- Agreeing and focusing on cross-cutting issues such as poverty, gender and participation.
- Planning for long-term capacity development and sustainability to make sure that the project adds to the empowerment and self-reliance of local people and institutions.
- Building in opportunities and actions that enhance learning and make possible adaptation of the project strategy during implementation.

These actions are crucial in planning, implementing and evaluating the building process of a community of learning in the complex environment of community health where, as we have seen, the educational focus are the major health problems of a country where graduates of the programmes function. The implications of this are that: (1) the content of the programmes does not only rest on the discipline that contributes to them, but also on the problems that characterize the programmes (2) the specific nature of the main health problems in a particular population differentiates one programme from another (3) as problems change from time to time, so also programmes are highly oriented to changes in the environment and (4) the student activities in the programmes should include issues in health education and promotion, disease prevention, health research and involvement of people in improvement of their health status.

As discussed, such an education must be a process that is transformative and developmental. Within an environmental plan, such education can take place at the various levels of an individual, organization, community and population. But in all instances the learning is conditional on engagement and is socially structured, and both formal and informal forms of learning are emphasized. As we have suggested, such education should rest on the Social Reconstructionism ideology which is grounded on the idea that education is a means of improving society. We have also indicated that in higher education communities, in which community members are committed to communicating with one another on an ever deeper and more authentic level, include communities of practice that involve groups of students, faculty and community members who work together, learn from each other and develop a common understanding of how to accomplish learning in a community. All these reflect the six good design practices of development interventions discussed earlier.

Many attempts to introduce educational interventions in community health have failed because such attempts have been made without due regard to such development practices. Why are these practices in building a community of learning for community health necessary? To begin with, many educational interventions in the community take some time to commence after initial design, during which the context will have changed. The development cycle usually includes many steps that lead to start-up, each of which takes time. Secondly, the initial design of the interventions may be attempted with limited time and resources. Many of the implementing partners will not have been identified and so there will have been limited participation in the process. This suggests a comprehensive participatory process of reviewing and, if need be, improving the design which is crucial at the beginning of the plan. After start-up, there are opportunities for improving the intervention design, such as on an annual basis as part of the annual progress review and planning process, and during the mid-term review.

The concept of self-reliance which is included in the six good practices in designing a development intervention is important to consider as it is one of the bases of effective community health development in many countries, especially in sub-Saharan Africa. In fact, the concept of self-reliance is located centrally within the discourse of community development and is connected to related concepts like self-help, mutual-help, indigenous participation and rural development. Self-help, for example, enables the local people to exploit to their advantage resources, which would otherwise lie dormant and thereby perpetuate the ignorance and poverty of their community, by making use of the under-utilized labour. For instance, self-help for community development can increase the competence and confidence of a community in handling its affairs.

Developing skills for self-help is a prerequisite for survival in the modern world (Galtung et al 1980, cited by Fonchingong et al 2003). Self-help initiatives enable the people to rally local resources and efforts for development. This is especially appropriate to the concept of community development, which stresses the importance of people increasing their sense of responsibility, and taking assistance as just supplementary, but never replacing popular initiatives or local efforts (e.g. Fonchingong et al 2003)). The emphasis is on democratizing with reliance on what people can do for themselves. The principle of self-help incorporates into the community development process the means of offering ordinary citizens the opportunity to share in making important decisions about their living conditions. This approach echoes the people-centredness of community development attempts at satisfying felt needs (e.g., Fonchingong et al 2003). This entails community participation at all levels of intervention development.

The self-reliance concept advocates the need for people to improve their physical, social and other conditions using local initiatives and resources available. Self-reliance is quickly being accepted as a new formula for community development (e.g. Fonchingong et al 2003). Its widespread acceptance in development planning of most African countries has the tendency to give greater stimulus and cohesiveness to community development in these countries (e.g. Fonchingong etal 2003). Self-reliance is now seen as an important point of take-off for better living. The emphasis is to involve groups of people in planned programmes from which they may gain skills that will enable them to cope more successfully with the problems of their everyday life. Self-reliance is therefore considered to be development on the basis of a country's (region's) own resources, involving its population based on the potential of its cultural values and traditions. Individuals, groups and communities define their own development according to their own needs, values and aspirations.

Another concept that also has much relevance for building a community of learning for community health and is, as can be seen, featured in the six good practices of any developmental intervention is sustainability. There are different views about what sustainability means and what can be done to foster it. Sustainability is generally seen as an economic, social and ecological concept, which is a means of configuring civilization and human activity (e.g. WCED 1987). It aims at providing for the best for humankind and the environment both now and in the future (e.g. WCED 1987).

The original term is sustainable development (UNCED 1992). Some experts now object to the term sustainable development as an umbrella term since it implies continued development that will cause great harm to humans in the future (UNCED 1992). In contrast, sustainability integrates environmental, economic and social concerns. Sustainability, then, is nowadays applied as a criterion to evaluate all aspects of human activity (UNCED 1992). Ben Eli (2005/2006), for example, proposes a somewhat different concept of sustainability as an organizing principle to enhance a well-functioning alignment between individuals, the economy, society and the regenerative capacity of the planet's life-supporting ecosystems. This alignment, according to Ben Eli, represents a specific kind of balance in the interaction between a population and the carrying capacity of its environment. Ben Eli suggests that it is this particular balance which must be the focus of a meaningful definition of sustainability. This concept of sustainability is based on five core principles that are expressed in relation to five fundamental domains shown in Box 8:

Box 8: Sustainability: Five Fundamental Domains

1. **The Material Domain:** Constitutes the basis for regulating the flow of materials and energy that underlie existence.
2. **The Economic Domain**: Provides a guiding framework for creating and managing wealth.
3. **The Domain of Life**: Provides the basis for appropriate behaviour in the biosphere.
4. **The Social Domain**: Provides the basis for social interactions.
5. **The Spiritual Domain**: Identifies the necessary attitudinal orientation and provides the basis for a universal code of ethics

---

Source: Ben Eli (2005/2006)

In economics, sustainable growth consists of increases in real incomes (i.e."inflation" -adjusted) or output that could be sustained for long periods of time (Department for the Environment, Food and Rural Affairs 2009). Therefore sustainable growth means, among other things, making profit. Social sustainability is concerned with the maintenance of social and human capital and keeping social and human capital intact. Human capital consists of knowledge, disposition, skills and expertise of people belonging to an organization. It is a source of creativity and innovation, and therefore of the competitive advantage of an organization (Woodcraft 2012).

In considering the concept of human capital increasing importance has now been given by theorists and analysts to the role of human learning within organizations and communities. Closely linked to the idea of learning or capital in organizations is the notion of social capital, which has gained importance among analysts in the current decade (OECD 2007)). Social capital refers to the components of social life, namely, the existence of networks, policies, institutions, relationships and norms (OECD 2007). A concept of social capital proposed by Putnam (1993) has three components, namely, moral obligations and norms, social values (particularly trust) and social networks (especially voluntary associations). The central tenet of this concept is that if a region successfully accumulates social capital it will have a well-functioning economic system and a high level of political integration. Another idea of social capital postulated by Bourdieu (1986) emphasizes conflicts and the power function- social relations that increase the ability of an actor to advance her/his interests. Also, Coleman (1988) explains the concept of social capital by identifying three forms of social capital: obligations and expectations which rest on the trustworthiness of the social environments, norms accompanied by sanctions, and information- flow capability of the social structure. According to Coleman (1988), the public good (a commodity or service that is provided without profit to all members of a society, either by the government or a private individual or organization) component of social capital is a characteristic shared by most forms of social capital. These aspects of social life enable people to act together, create synergies and build partnerships.

There is a link between human and social capital. Social capital can influence the ability to acquire human capital through, for example, the enhancement of learning at school by strong communities (OECD 2007). Also, in order to preserve social capital for sustained economic growth and development it is necessary to foster networks of trust and knowledge creation and sharing at the organizational, community and regional levels, as well as between different sectors, such as government, higher education and business (OECD 2005). Goodland et al (1996) argue that social capital requires the maintenance and replenishment of shared values by communities, social and religious groups.

Within the wider health sector, sustainability has become synonymous with self-sufficiency in financing and often applied to situations where external aid agencies sought to induce developing country governments to take on the responsibility for funding activities that previously had been donor funded (Levine et al 2001). However it is now generally agreed that both domestic and external funding are necessary for sustaining public health programme. Thus, the concepts of self-reliance and sustainability and the other ideas in the education of health professionals for the community are consistent with the democratic principles of participation, cooperation, empowerment, capacity building, etc., which define the concepts of community health and PHC and provide conceptual understanding of community-oriented education for health professionals.

The following sections further focus on the leadership, management and educational approaches that can promote these community development ideas and processes in relation to community-oriented education of health professionals, starting with the important issue of how to deal with resistance to organizational change.

Resistance to Organisational Change

One issue that the innovator must deal with is the problem of resistance to organizational change, which is well documented in the social science and health literature.. For example, Barrows (1997) in an article entitled "The problems and responsibilities of leadership in educational innovations" suggests that innovators should disseminate the innovation, which he considers the most problematic and most crucial of the innovator's responsibilities. He presents three problems. Citing "The Prince" by Machiavelli, Barrows describes the first problem as resistance to organizational change:

"it must be considered that there is nothing more difficult to carry out, nor more doubtful of success, nor more dangerous to handle, than to initiate a new order of things."

As we have seen in Chapter 7, a strong influence that affects decisions about the healthcare educational institutions is history or tradition. Head teachers and their teachers have been schooled in certain ways with regard to the subject they teach and the teaching methods they use, which are difficult to change. Doing so will mean that they will have to begin all over again- to learn new ways of teaching and forgo the confidence which teaching a subject provides, or using certain techniques with which they feel secure and in which they are sure of their knowledge and capability. This, to a large extent, seemingly accounts for the resistance to organizational change.

There is a good deal of evidence in the literature relating to organizational change to show that social scientists, in attempting to look for the success or failure of planned organizational change have tended mainly to see the problem as that of defeating the initial resistance to change. Consequently, many explanations of the success or failure of such a change by social scientists direct their attention towards the capability of a manager or change agent to defeat initial resistance to change.

The reasoning behind the initial resistance to change concept seems to be connected to Leavitt's 'power equalization concept', cited by Gross et al (1971), which many social scientists claim can account for differences in organizational success in implementing change. This explanation supposes that members of an organization who must implement an innovation will want to resist it unless they have been made part of the formulation process of the innovation in the first place. Furthermore, it assumes that such resistance comprises the fundamental difficulty in the implementation of the innovation. Therefore, in order to overcome resistance management must share its power with those who must implement innovation by allowing them to take part in the decision-making process of the change to be made. Additionally, it is supposed that individuals who are to implement the innovation will, as a result, see the innovation as self-imposed and hence become committed to it.

The topic of resistance to change is also given importance in the literature on group dynamics. Social scientists have declared that by using human relations schemes in sensitivity groups, resisting the change by organizational members can be neutralized and a positive adjustment to change can be installed.

However, Gross et al argue that these statements have overlooked certain critical considerations about organizational change:

1. obstacles to which members who are not resistant to change may be exposed when they make efforts to implement innovations,
2. the possible role that management, in working with subordinates may play in creating or overcoming these obstacles,
3. the possibility that members who are not initially resistant to an organizational change may later develop a negative attitude to it.

Gross et al conclude that there is a need for social scientists to recognize the necessity of conceptualizing the success or failure of the implementation of organizational innovations as the result of a complex set of interrelated forces that occur over an extended period of time after the innovation has been introduced. They therefore suggest the need for in-depth look at organizations like schools, trying to implement organizational innovations in order to isolate factors which inhibit and facilitate the implementation of innovations. Important constraints that are likely to operate within the school that the innovator must deal with can be listed under these three headings: (1) difficulties created by human aspects, such as the level of interest teachers have in the innovation, (2) resource constraints, such as class sizes and (3), administrative constraints, such as the kind of discipline that exists in an educational institution. For example, in reviewing medical programmes in Mexico, Nicaragua and Costa Rica, Braveman et al (1987) found in all programmes a widespread problem of resistance of some faculty, particularly affiliated faculty, to the new direction, or lack of preparation to teach new material and methods. In addition, there was shortage of finances which reflected in limitation in faculty development, research and faculty-student interaction. The programmes reviewed were representative of the range of types and degrees of innovations among institutions that have participated in the reform movement in Latin America to orient medical education to community health and PHC.

The responsibilities of the innovator in the investigation of such factors become more crucial when one considers that resistance to organizational change takes considerable time, which Barrows says is the next problem faced by the innovator in educational institutions. According to Barrows, whether or not there is encouragement for the innovation and its use, and evaluation by others, such resistance lasts a long time. Barrows suggests 20 years as the period resistance to an innovation could last. Schools tend to adopt ideas about twenty to twenty-five years after they first become available. Even after this time the resistance could persist despite the innovation being successful and widely used.

Factors fostering acceptance or rejection of innovation can be placed under two main categories. One category consists of factors that influence the contract likely acceptors have with the innovation, including awareness of its characteristics and the behaviour needed for its implementation. The other category comprises forces that relate to the compatibility of the innovation with the culture of the people to whom the innovation is introduced. Thus, another important influence that team leaders trying to implement innovation and change must deal with is the climate of the organization.

Organizational Climate

The climate of an organization can be characterized on the basis of the behaviour of people in a particular organization. Educational institutions, for example, differ greatly in their climate. While some of these institutions are alive with ideas and interest, others maintain a more conventional way of doing things. The institutions where there is much interest and ideas are characterized by several aspects (Miles 1975): the goals of the organization are clear to members and relatively well received by them; information is well distributed; the influence of members is fairly equally distributed, thereby making the influence of subordinates felt at upper levels of the organization; resources, especially personal resources, are used effectively; there is a sense of identity and a feeling of well-being among members, rather than disappointment; there is movement towards new goals, and new procedures are created; the organization is comparatively autonomous and independent of outside influences; and the structure of the organization is steadily adopting to accommodate new demands.

Additionally, there is an effective system that copes sufficiently with problems. The role of the leader of the team, who as head of the institution has conventional authority and enjoys a total view of the organization, entails leadership which deals with the introduction of new policies and ideas. This role is critically important as his style of leadership will affect the climate of the organization. Equally important is his style of decision-making. Although the decision-making style the leader uses may depend on a given situation, ideally the leader should allow other staff to share the decision-making process and agrees with the collective decision. The leader works very hard; he is flexible and ready to formulate rules and judge if necessary. He considers staff needs important and does not monitor staff too closely, especially staffs that are capable. He tries to ensure that relationships are good and staff morale is high. The decision – making role of the leader in creating the right climate for curriculum innovation and change is therefore very crucial.Decision-making Process.

In the context of a cultural analysis-type curriculum, this means that the team-leader as innovator, as well as the school's teaching staff, must have a clear idea of the aims of the innovation, in this case, the common curriculum proposed, its benefits as well as its effectiveness. This will require discussions on all aspects of the curriculum, including curriculum models, teaching/learning strategies, procedures and methods, including methods of evaluating its effectiveness. The levels at which such discussion can take place may differ from one institution to another depending on factors such as the size of the organization. For example (Lawton 1983), there can be three levels at which such discussion can be usefully conducted in school committees. The first level deals with coverage and balance for the curriculum as a whole and should be led by the head of school. The aim will be to ensure cooperation of all departments in total curriculum planning. The second level will seek to maximize co-ordination and co-operation within the departments. Here, the departmental head will chair the proceedings. The third level committee will discuss matters concerning inter-departmental integration for the purpose of fostering better co-ordination and co-operation between departments.

One of the justifications for integration is that a rearrangement of the content of the curriculum according to some cross- disciplinary theme quite often results in changing the content itself, new ideas being added and others reduced. It is hence a means of stimulating constructive dialogues among instructors and for revising a curriculum.

The objective of these three levels of committees and discussion is to ensure that all members of staff are involved, and feel that they are involved, and have a real opportunity for voicing their own particular points of view. This principle, as we have seen, is important in creating an ideal organizational climate for innovation and change However, for the purposes of planning PHC/community health education a much wider structure of committees- a multidisciplinary/interdisciplinary team structure- seems more appropriate than the above arrangement alone. Possible planning structures that are based on the multidisciplinary health team approach should be explored by the innovator (and his faculty team) and must include, in addition to the teaching teams, other stakeholders such as external experts, advisers, representatives of the UN and other agencies, NGOs, students, etc. Any useful persons can be included in the team, if the innovator and his faculty find it necessary.

In fact, the innovator and his faculty team can consider the possibility of having the three levels of school committees run parallel with the multidisciplinary team, or search for other more suitable ways the two structures can be harmonized. Table 13 below presents an example of participatory processes of curriculum development frameworks that reflect this and other possibilities. The framework is outlined in a case study description (Tenn et al 1994) of a contractual collaboration between various stakeholders in post-graduate programmes based on primary health care. Such frameworks can be adopted or used as a basis for discussion on possible curriculum development processes that can most effectively follow the multidisciplinary team approach and produce the best results.

As the table shows, there were several major spheres of influence or systems that participated in the process of consultation and collaboration in the development and evaluation of the curriculum project. These included stakeholders that funded the curriculum development project, consisting of WHO (to implement and provide technical and human resources), United Nations Population Fund (UNFPA) (principal funding agency) and the Government. Other participating stakeholders were practising nurses, educators, administrators, students, community leaders, other health sectors representatives, an education consultant, and an advisory committee. The actual development of the curriculum itself was undertaken by a core-group consisting of the coordinator of the course, public health nursing supervisors, the education consultant and public health nurses. The core-group was guided and advised concerning curriculum development by an advisory committee made up of 15 health personnel: educators, nursing administrators, medical officers, health inspectors, health educators, and health statistics and planning personnel. The main function of the advisory committee was to communicate divergent views, to make sure that the programme was relevant, making decisions on issues on which there were disagreements, granting vito to suggestions, and lobbying for acceptance of the programme at the development stage. At the evaluation stage, a renewed advisory committee, consisting mainly of nurses, served as the channel through which the process was approved and data findings renewed. Nurses (professionals) involvement was ensured by including at different stages in the development and evaluation process practising nurses in health care settings in urban and rural areas who, on the basis of their practical experience, were able to identify numerous learning needs. They were able to provide the realities of public health practice and give information about the relevance of the programme and their expectations in terms of public health practice. They also provided data regarding the implementation of the programme.

Table 13: Participatory Process of Curriculum Development

Community Groups	Core group & Advisory Committee	Public Health Nurses In Practice & Nursing Leaders
Health needs, beliefs and practices; expectations and responsibilities of PHN in community.	Responsible for project; knowledge of Tongan society, health needs and government policies; tailoring of course to Tongan needs; decisions on points of contention	Definitionn of present practice, expectations and aspiration. Task analysis, individual and group definition of new practice and needed knowledge, attitudes and skills

Representatives from Health/Other Sectors	Definition of knowledge, attitudes, skills and aspirations pertinent to the practice of Public Health Nursing in Tonga	Public Health Nurses as Learners
Health: medical officers, health officers, health educators, trained birth attendants, village health workers. Groups in other sectors: agriculture, environment, non-governmental agencies. Expectations, relationship patterns; Intersectoral collaboration.		Basic nursing school curriculum patterns of additional training. Nurses' characteristics profile. Self-identification of individual needs.

Agency Stakeholders	Consultant	Government of the kingdom of Tonga
WHO: Concept of primary health care and of safe motherhood. UNFPA: Concept of strengthening community information, motivation and participant in family planning.	Partner in process: knowledge of curriculum development and content; coordinating link between stakeholders; proposing strategies & plans; translating myriad of perspectives into coherent whole acceptable to approving bodies.	**Major Stakeholder** Decision-making power: Approval of project and implementation. Development plan: health policies manpower and health legislation. Other specialized training programmes

Source: Tenn et al (1994)

Whatever its composition, the effectiveness of the multidisciplinary team (and, or school committees) will depend on team members' knowledge about one another and each other's role in the team. In addition, it will be necessary to address questions about how the chairman or team leader is decided upon (if he is not the school or department head), and the qualities he or she requires. Other questions that relate to the team's effectiveness must also demand the attention of the innovator. One is the issue of who makes which decision, which has been already dealt with. It is, however, necessary to stress that an early decision on possibilities, such as the course team making all decisions by consensus after discussing the issues involved is crucial if discord is to be minimized in the future. Another question is how the work should be shared. Here again, an early decision is important. Unless this is done some are bound to do more than others, and most important, crucial tasks may be left undone. Furthermore, questions about the nature of schedule and how to communicate within the team are important. On the issue of schedule, the need to agree on a production timetable so that team members will know when this work is anticipated is crucial.

There are two important requirements here. One is to allot enough time for serious reading of one another's work or getting comments from reviewers. The other is the need for contingency planning in the event course planning or production is late. Concerning methods of communication, what must firstly be considered is the need to get all the members of the team, who not all may know each other, to accept and trust each other, as already mentioned. This will require meetings that will purely be businesslike, such as brainstorming or discussion sessions, professional; like workshops; social events such as parties; or a mixture of all three. Whatever the type of meeting, the aim must be to foster acquaintance between members and getting the work done. The crucial decisions on all aspects of the work must be documented and made available to members. Each and every member or group should circulate to other members descriptions of the parts of the work they have been assigned. All members must also have the opportunity to view and to comment on any material that may have a bearing on the planning of their individual or group assignments. To facilitate this kind of curriculum development, the innovator must explore ways of dealing with the problem of resistance to organizational change in particular situations, such as those Barrows offers for tackling such a problem: disseminate, promote and advertise the innovation.

Other possible measures that the innovator can employ include strategies to cause change to be seen as advantageous by according titles to members of an organization, sheer persuasive skills, or by financial incentives. The fact that the planning of, among other things, cross-disciplinary instruction requires considerable time and efforts underscores the significance of proper dispensation of this responsibility. For instance, the enormous difficulties in changing an existing curriculum, rigidly filled with subjects, to a cultural analysis-based common curriculum, indicated to be compulsory, points up this very time-consuming exercise. In this process the innovator should consider how to apply related strategic guidelines in the best way possible. One of such guidelines is, as already mentioned, inviting people from outside the school, particularly other members of the multidisciplinary health team, to assist in curriculum planning. The other guideline has also been recommended, again on the basis of experience and research evidence. This is involving more people in curriculum planning, so that they will work harder to make the plan successful. However, despite their usefulness in curriculum innovation and change, the application of these 'principles', especially the second one, can lead to unproductive outcomes if not followed with caution. Bringing more people into a discussion often does not increase the number of good ideas because big groups may not necessarily produce creativity. Because of this, the innovator may consider also using where appropriate another approach to these management techniques that pledges to generate innovative strategies and set in motion workers' interests through investing heavily in selection and training of staff to create the kind of strong-willed individual who (instead of directing people who have the most interesting things to say) will be able to rely on his or her judgment for big strategic decisions. This proposal should however not mean that the innovator should ignore the democratic concepts and principles of PHC. Here it mainly suggests the necessity of giving careful thought to the membership, structure and other characteristics of curriculum planning groups, the importance of the skills and leadership qualities of the manager or innovator, and the aim of the education that will provide such skills and qualities for effective curriculum planning in the contexts of the cultural analysis planning approach and PHC/Community health.

Continuing Education

Continuing education is a very necessary factor in this curriculum development endeavour. Clearly, such curriculum development will also make particular demands on the expertise and skills of teachers, among other things, and the responsibility of the innovator in developing teachers and others concerned (clinical staff, supervisors, etc) cannot be over-emphasized. Perhaps nowhere is the saying that there cannot be effective curriculum development without teacher development truer than in the business of planning a cultural analysis and PHC/Community Health-type curriculum. The innovator must provide the opportunities that will ensure that the necessary skills and expertise are developed or reinforced through school – based and community-based in-service and other continuing education programmes. They must, in particular, be prepared for the new roles the integrated curriculum, the process curriculum model, problem-solving and multi-professional approaches, together with the new teaching/learning principles, strategies and approaches, will create. The significance of such continuing education becomes clearer when it is looked at especially in relation to the curriculum process model which, as mentioned earlier, rests on teacher judgment rather than on teacher direction. It is far more demanding on teachers and therefore far more difficult to implement in practice, (although it offers a high degree of personal and professional development). In specific circumstances it may well prove too demanding. There are also difficulties in assessment of students that the process model poses, such as exposure of the strengths and weaknesses of teachers. This calls for development of the teacher's skills and understanding of the concept so that he can appreciate the value of the curriculum process concept and be able and willing to participate actively in its implementation, including assessment on which it is based. The same applies to the concepts of the integrated curriculum, common curriculum, the problem-solving approach, and education for work. The knowledge and skills of teachers must be developed in terms of awareness of the characteristics of these concepts and the behaviour needed for their implementation. This must include not only knowledge about the concepts and skills for using them, but also social and political skills such as negotiation, co-operation, advocacy, lobbying, etc., – skills that are absent in many training curricula of health professionals and have been identified in the selection from culture in Chapter 6. The aim of such continuing education should be to enable the teachers to influence decisions that can bring about changes in structural arrangements, expenditure patterns, organizational, and administrative structures that are needed for implementing the change effectively. For example, the task of rostering duplicate class enrolment of a large number of students into a technology laboratory with inadequate seats is an example of the problems associated with insufficiency of physical resources that requires considerable negotiating patience and skill on the part of teachers and the team leader. Indeed, in many agencies that were responsible for initiating change, the most crucial influence on success was that the Head teacher had undertaken courses on leadership and managing change. Such courses were responsible for providing the initial impetus for some of the innovations. Such continuing education, like curriculum development, must be school or community-based. As such they provide the innovator opportunities for linking closely curriculum development with teacher development, and development of their collaborators. It is therefore preferred to sending, for example, staff abroad for curriculum development-related further education. However, in order to facilitate strategy formulation the innovator can also consider the need for new ways of thinking in curriculum planning and, thus, the necessity of sending managers or innovators abroad or to other places outside schools sometimes to gain new perspectives.

Resources

The Resource Dependence Theory (Pfeffer et al 1978) is basically about power, keeping it and maintaining it. It suggests that the primary motivator for organizational behaviour is the desire to reduce uncertainty about getting the resources necessary to operate (these resources are usually financial but may also include key personnel, seats on influential community boards, or persons opposed to effort at getting the needed resources who are with prestigious organizations).

To be effective, community health faculty leaders must be able to accurately analyze power issues both within an agency and within the community. They must be able to predict the resource requirements of the agency and how managing those resources may affect power issues within the system. For the purpose of community-oriented education of health professionals, examples of important resources include space, budgets, staff, equipment, and community agencies and groups. Faculty leaders must try to ensure that they have adequate resources to achieve their mission, vision, and goals for educating health professionals in the community.

In addition to making specific demands on the expertise and skills of teachers, school or community-based curriculum development will raise questions on resources limitations. Innovations demand energy and finance, not to mention, among other things, the time of health workers who have to deal with the problem of work overload in the communities where students are supervised. There are also other resource constraints of a more practical nature and of more organizational importance, such as the considerable time and energy community-based teaching/learning requires. Criticisms from students and tutorial staff undergoing community health experiences reflect such financial, technical and managerial problems that relate to resource limitations. There are often problems such as difficulty in finding accommodation for staff and students in the community, lack or shortage of money to pay for lodging and boarding in the community, inadequate supervisors for students, difficulty in getting into a routine as students sometimes move from one village to another, for example, every two to three weeks, lack of transport to get to villages students are assigned as a result of logistical constraints such as fuel shortage, difficulty to get to know members of the community, especially if they are from a different ethnic group from the student, and lack of interest from district or divisional health teams, who may complain of not being able to supervise students because of shortage of staff and fuel. There are also inadequate or lack of much needed teaching and learning materials, supplies and equipment/facilities such as communication facilities in the community including telephones.

To deal with these resource issues, the innovator should consider the proper kind of outside assistance teachers require to satisfy curriculum development requirements. In fact, we must stress the need for the leader and teachers to consider in their planning the search for possible material resources developed by others inside the school (e.g., by staff of other departments), or outside the school (e.g., a workable method (Marsenich 1983), of teaching the steps of change: awareness, understanding, acceptance and change, or models of moral education), and using human resources from outside the school (e.g., an able political scientist), rather than trying to work out such requirements themselves, which may not produce the best results, often waste time, and will not allow for the necessary and useful co-operation that working with others, particular other members of the multidisciplinary team, provides in terms of relevant knowledge, skills and attitude development. As can be seen from Table 7 above, the participatory processes of curriculum development Ten et al describe also include individuals and/or groups in the community that can usefully participate in curriculum planning. The team leader and teachers should analyze the financial, technical and managerial aspects of policy with a view to assessing the accessibility of resources, and to judging how resources can be assembled to guarantee increased practical implementation of policy. The key is to assemble such resources to strengthen policy reforms. As we noted in an earlier discussion, people who are not resistant to change, may subsequently encounter difficulties that will constrain their efforts to implement change. It is clear from that discussion that sufficient or appropriately channelled financial resources (from 1st and 2nd levels mainly), and managerial resources, such as practical information and a sound administrative system are crucial factors when implementing a curriculum policy reform. In fact, efforts aimed at implementing policy reforms have shown that changes in policy were most often reported from countries with high economic development. Therefore, governments and curriculum innovators in poor countries should explore the possibility of securing support from funding mechanisms that can greatly enhance relevant curriculum policy implementation, such as the one used by WHO (Jancloes 1998) to develop an intensified approach for cooperation with countries and people in greatest need in order to improve the implementation of primary health care. This approach includes preliminary missions to countries, consultations with international agencies and joint missions with multilateral and bilateral cooperating agencies, material and technical assistance through WHO Regional Offices, and earmarking of funds to enable WHO technical programmes to focus attention on selected countries.

The Policy and Political Environment

All these also call for looking at how the innovator can prepare for problems that are likely to emanate from the policy and political arena, such as potential opposition to the innovation and lack of sufficient support for the innovation. Already, there is a well-developed policy in healthcare in two respects (Boaden et al 1999). One aspect is professional representation to governments and other agencies to advance their interests. Professionals have been successful in this endeavour, but the political processes involved are becoming harder, hence there is a need to change the ability or skills of the professional health worker. The other aspect is the area of public/community health where specialist doctors do not treat patients and have comparatively little to do with many of the health workers who provide direct health care to communities. Their principal role lies in modifying public and institutional behaviour in ways that agree with prevention of disease and promotion of health. They have been doing this work for a long time; however, the influence they command require high understanding and skills in policy and decision – making processes, and processes of institutional operations. Furthermore, the type of reward which comes from the cure and alleviation of patients' conditions and their patients' appreciation is reduced in the PHC system, because the link between health professionals' efforts and the health of the people is less clear. As we mentioned earlier, there is often a hierarchical order in the health system that rests on prestige and power between the different medical traditions. This situation often results in more powerful traditions (eg medical doctors) exploiting or suppressing feeble traditions (e.g., traditional healers).

As also mentioned above, the aim of the needed continuing education should be to enable the team leader and teachers to influence decisions that can bring about changes in structural arrangements, expenditure patterns, organizational, and administrative structures that are needed for implementing the curriculum policy effectively. The processes of consultation in such efforts are often quite unusual for the majority of health professionals and the close association between those involved can bring about traditional behaviours linked to hierarchy. Therefore, establishing trust, respect and egalitarian partnership can be a long and difficult process. The innovator trying to get communities to participate in planning and implementation of curriculum policy may have to deal with many constraints, such as professional monopolization of health services leading to loss in community participation. Learning to tackle such difficulties will help the leader and teachers increase and strengthen their teaching capacity, as well as serve as a role model to their students in the teaching and learning process.

Let us take as an example the common curriculum idea. As already mentioned, this idea should not be confused with the policy of having a uniform curriculum. The common curriculum idea demands that planners decide on the concepts and experiences which will give access to worthwhile knowledge and make it possible for all students to access this minimum programme. Some students will certainly progress much further, while some will fall behind in the basic understanding of the common programme. However, all students will have been given access to useful knowledge, such as Eraut's three different forms of knowledge that underpin professional education. Moreover, it should not, as mentioned earlier, mean the controlling of education from the outside through demands for requirements like objectives.

However, this understanding is not always possible because of the divergent views, or lack of universal agreement, even among teachers, on what education is all about, including ideas on education that rest on the common curriculum idea. It is clear that national debates on the common curriculum, like education ideas in general, emanate from the fact that those involved in the debate are addressing it from various viewpoints. Such differences lead to various practical proposals which may be a major source of chaos. This, to some extent, may account for the lack of success and frustrations, even where the principle of a common curriculum has been accepted. For example, the literature review on the subject of inter-disciplinary education of health care professionals (Stephenson et al 2002), as mentioned earlier, also shows that while many healthcare professionals agree that including interdisciplinary experiences in education is crucial for improvement of health care delivery, reforms to implement such education in the form of, for example, the common curriculum have been slow and universities have dealt with the challenges of implementation to various degrees with different strategies. Therefore, the innovator should let officials higher up in the hierarchy, including ministry of health officials that often include health professionals, as well as participating community health workers at lower levels of implementation, have a good knowledge of the innovation and its meaning, and trying to secure additional support and input from such important persons for the innovation. Indeed, by Barrows' (1997) own account "the innovator should never pass on the opportunity to present the innovation to educational and medical specialty organizations nationally or internationally"- another not too easy way by which the innovator can prepare for the problems of successful leadership. The difficulties of such a task become more apparent when one considers that there may be significant cultural differences and disjunctions of loyalty between government officials working in national offices, who are distanced from the realities at the local levels, and governmental officers working at the local level. Walt (1994) argues that there is considerable complicity between the two cultures, so that the language of the official culture is used to justify decisions which satisfy the implicit culture.

According to Walt, this is a good reason why, though certain policies coming from the Ministry of Health may be implemented, they often do not realize their objectives like improving health care. It is in such political situations that accountability questions concerning the functions of schools are likely to be raised. Clearly, one of the functions of the school system is to produce the manpower a country needs and this is a factor that cannot be ignored in curriculum planning. In health care, this kind of argument points to demands for a good education of health personnel who are able and willing to serve the community by providing health care, promoting health, preventing disease and caring for those in need. As mentioned in Chapter 4, the cultural analysis model as well as the other curriculum planning models discussed in Chapter 3, have been criticized for failing to consider the requirements and opinions of service managers/ employers on the outputs they need for education and training to meet their service contracts. In considering the relevance of the models/systems of accountability (Chapter 7) and Lawton's ideal types of evaluation (Chapter 9) to cultural analysis, Lawton suggests that the democratic model of accountability and the evaluation types of estimates of teacher competence, briefing decision-makers, teacher as researcher and case study have more in common with cultural analysis than the other evaluation models. When criteria of cultural analysis are applied to the issue of accountability, cultural analysis methods would suggest that it is necessary to look at schools in a broader way and to establish goals on a wider scale than only preparation for employment. As he says, it is important to look at the question of school efficiency not simply from one angle but from a variety of cultural view points, using a complete cultural analysis approach. But he points out that it is more useful to include external moderators, which may include managers/employers, in self-evaluation of schools than employing simple methods of evaluating the efficiency of schools on the basis of testing/examination. We have seen that those who are accountable in the effort to educate health professionals must register success in public exams in a significant manner. Moreover, exams, particularly external exams, are used for the accountability of teachers. However, as already mentioned, accountability should not be viewed as support for such prescriptions for tests/examinations.

Thus, accountability in schools, often seen as essential for efficient management, supervision and direction, tends to stress testing when applied to curriculum content. When applied to curriculum content, accountability tends to stress three components: (1) more focus on basic skills, (2) examination results and warnings to publish league tables, and (3) coercion to make the curriculum more vocational and stressing links between schools and industry (Lawton 1983). But cultural analysis shows that a much more open approach to looking at knowledge or content is required than this narrow view.

It is clear from the discussion in Chapter 7 that the democratic model of accountability is the model that can provide this open approach and the alternate schemes of accountability that can meet the needs of the cultural analysis-type common curriculum. It has the benefit of acknowledging that the business of education is by far more sophisticated than the defenders of the bureaucratic model seem to believe. Most importantly, it is compatible with the cultural analyses approach to curriculum planning and the PHC/Community health principles we highlighted in the foregoing discussion, for not only does it recognize the rights of teachers to be involved directly in the process of accountability and to consult their colleagues in such a process, it also recognizes the need for teachers to forge links between the various stakeholders and all those concerned with social and health development. In deed, in describing a framework for defining and measuring the social accountability of medical schools Boelen et al (1995), for example, suggest that the main stakeholders in health care should decide to work together and should agree on the basic values of relevance (the degree to which the most important health problems are tackled first), quality (health care that uses evidence-based data and appropriate technology to deliver comprehensive health care to individuals and populations, taking into account their social, cultural and consumer expectations), cost-effectiveness (health care systems that have the greatest impact on the health of a society while making the best use of its resources) and equity (striving towards making high-quality health care available to all people in all countries) which are implicit in the goal of "Health for All", which provides such a foundation.

The difficulties of structuring applicable schemes of accountability should serve as a challenge that teachers must face with enthusiasm; they should not allow such constraints to become sources of discouragement and/or frustration. Teachers must acknowledge the intricacies of education and endeavour to formulate equally complex but effective schemes of evaluation and accountability rather than cheapen their work to the over simplistic level that current schemes use to evaluate. Evaluation frameworks, such as the one proposed by Boelen et al (1995) for self-evaluation of the social accountability of medical schools can be considered for use by teachers after evaluating their appropriateness and acceptability.

However, it is worth making another point about accountability which is that accountability of the teacher should be received, not rejected. The reason for this is that, apart from totalitarian states, people living in democratic societies must be accountable for their behaviour or deeds. This deals with the responsibility and acknowledging that responsibility in some public way. As has been mentioned, teachers as citizens are obligated to obey the laws of the countries they are part of but, additionally, they are legally accountable to their heads and employers, only to these two legally. There is no contractual relationship between teachers and their students. This moral obligation can be perceived as a form of accountability by teachers. Furthermore, as teachers may see it, such moral obligation may be more important than whatever legal contract they have. However, factors such as reduction of resources to education, which create limits to the teacher's work, make it difficult to identify the things that teachers can be called to account for. The head of an institution is legally accountable to his controlling body and to the education authority. However, he is morally accountable to his teachers and students. Head teachers, for instance, make crucial decisions on the allocation of resources and must therefore be accountable to a large extent for the work of the schools. Teachers as professionals in academic institutions who are charged with the task of developing an intellectual culture and meeting the manpower needs of countries, ought to enjoy operational autonomy (with respect to aspects such as administration, staffing, operations, curriculum standards, and accounts). However, such autonomy is not unlimited; indeed it is restrained by the overriding need to conduct business responsibly which requires objectivity, sensitivity to societal interest and action within the framework of the rule of law and the democratic cultures of countries.

The role of the communication media in the process of accountability requires consideration as attitudes to education are greatly influenced by the ethos of society, which to a large extent is created by the mixed influences of, among other things, the communication media that is usually connected to it. As has been mentioned (Chapter 7), the media can draw the attention of governments to issues and pressure governments to take action, or not to do so on a health issue, and those aspects of the communication media like television programmes can overthrow rather than defend the work of schools. Therefore, in order to establish its credibility, the innovator must advertise the innovation in the media as early as possible, after having initially evaluated it. The motto "publish or perish" couldn't be truer for the innovator.

Also important in the accountability process is conducting research to further support the development and assessment of the innovation. This may arguably be agood way to mobilize resources, bring added reputation to the school, and increase the innovator's defence. However, the innovator must realize that there is often no direct or immediate link between evaluation and research and policy. There are many other factors that determine the extent to which research and evaluation can influence policy. The process of use will be affected by the nature and intimacy of the links between policy makers and researchers, and the role the media play in research dissemination. Use of research will depend on the timing and mode of communication. In addition, research or evaluations being taken seriously and used by policy makers will rest on political or ideological factors, conceptual confusion and uncertainty about research results and uncertainty about the usefulness of research (Walt (1994). Giving due attention to such constraints, such as inviting policy makers to scientific sessions at which research objectives and results are presented and discussed will certainly improve policy- makers' regard for and use of research.

We must make this final point about accountability. The issue of accountability will be critical for developing a PHC/Community health and cultural analysis oriented curriculum. The more one adheres to the democratic model of accountability the more one will allow for a school-based or community-based curriculum development that will be more successful. It will involve a greater measure of autonomy for teachers and liberty to modify and alter the curriculum without the constraints on such effort we identified in the above discussion. Furthermore, it will involve a greater measure of professional involvement. The autonomy of teachers can result in better methods and procedures for accountability, not less.

Identification of difficulties on curriculum policy implementation and addressing such problems is often a much needed measure to facilitate execution of curriculum policy, whether or not local officials consent to implementation of a policy. Here, the innovator can usefully adopt a five-component model (Gadomski et al 1990) to examine certain constraints in policy execution:

inputs: the boundary of technology with field conditions can produce difficulties, for example, difficulties in using certain teaching strategies/methods in the communities students are attached for practical experience, due to factors such as lack of electricity, etc.,

process: policy execution will necessitate interchange between communities, health workers and other groups. Factors like indifferent attitudes to people's feelings and disrespect for people's cultures may result in unsuccessful policy implementation;

outputs: instead of enumerating exact outputs, outputs that represent the effective utilization by those who use resources are a more valid assessment of benefits. However, effective use of resources usually demands changes in behaviour, which are difficult to achieve in the difficult conditions in many communities, particularly in developing countries;

outcome: access to those in need of care and groups at high-risk are the things that should indicate effectiveness in health care delivery. This is because the localities in which such groups reside and their socio-cultural and economic backgrounds make it difficult for them to access health facilities, or for health workers to reach them and;

impact: several problems persist at the final stage of health care execution, such as biological difficulties that reduce the impact health care can make in limiting immorality. The causes of death are so numerous and conflicting for one to be able to tackle them all. Thus one successful health intervention like the common curriculum cannot prevent the possible death of a child from an assembly of other problems. This is why to trace the long-term impact of health training schools variables such as clinical skills, attitudes towards patients and carrier projections to various aspects of the curriculum have been studied.

Certain features of curriculum policy may also foster or hinder implementation. A policy with relatively simple technical features is much easier to initiate than a complex policy because a policy with complex features may require new knowledge and technology, in addition to compliance, which may be difficult to achieve. If a policy needs just a marginal change from existing situations or circumstances, the risk of mistakes are minimized, cost, including capital costs, are smaller, so also is the amount of information required. If a policy is implemented by one actor (e.g. Ministry of Health) and does not hang on co-ordination and collaboration with other officials, executioners will have more control of the implementation. This, as we mentioned earlier, should not be a sufficient condition for effective execution and should not be given precedence over collaboration and co-ordination. So also will the implementation likely run more easily if the goals of the policy are clearly stated, as already mentioned, and if there is one major goal. Finally, if the implementation is conducted in a short period of time it will have a better chance of succeeding, as it will be unlikely to suffer from change in leadership, the problem of new actors taking part in the execution, and organized resistance (Walt 1994).

If effective curriculum policy implementation is to be achieved, efforts must be put into dealing with such socio-cultural, economic and political issues. In this regard, there are two concepts in policy implementation that are worthy of consideration by the innovator: impact and visibility of policy. As explained by (Walt 1994), if the cost or burden of reform is felt strongly by the public, or the strong interest groups, opposition will emerge during implementation. Reforms that impose broadly dispersed costs directly on the public also frequently generate benefits that are not widely understood or appreciated. The visibility of the reform may affect public reaction too. If a policy change does not require major administrative resources or high technical skills to sustain it, it is more likely to be implemented. Thus the public may benefit over the long term from the creation of a PHC system but the direct impact is originally borne by officials, health managers and professionals who have to change old habits and institutional rules and relinquish accustomed forms of security, control and responsibility. If opposition arises in the bureaucracy, implementation may be delayed or even arrested. Administrators are likely to understand the cost long before the public recognizes the benefits, and unless policy makers can mobilize some countervailing support for the policy in the public arena, it is unlikely that the policy will be implemented as intended Thus, the team leader and teachers should also analyze the political aspects of policy with the aim to assessing the accessibility of resources, and to judging how resources can be assembled to guarantee increased practical implementation of policy. Failure to do this on their part is a weakness in implementation. To analyze the political resources, there are four questions (Walt 1994) that the innovator and his team need to answer to judge whether it is necessary to assemble additional resources: "How legitimate is the regime? Is this a single, one-off policy change, or part of many different (and unpopular) changes? How autonomous is the government? Is there a consensus among the elites in favour of policy change? How far do elites share the government's perception of the problem? Answers to such questions will help the innovators contemplate the nature of potential political support or resistance to the policy. As we have seen, groups with common interests such as professional teacher groups are likely to oppose a policy that conflicts with their professional interests. We have also seen that levels of literacy can influence the way people comprehend and utilize information, including information on policy change. Additionally, as has been indicated, assessing the usefulness of policy change can also help policy makers assemble political forces that approve of the policy reform All these require consideration of using the mass media whose influence on the processes of health policy, as we noted earlier in Chapter 7, is usually underrated. Because their communicative sphere of use or functions is very extensive, the innovator can use both the print and electronic media to communicate curriculum policy and to obtain the needed resources and other kinds of support for curriculum policy implementation. As we mentioned above, the mass media can have many functions, such as serving as information providers and tools for propaganda; and they can be used as instruments of genuineness, originating plurality of beliefs in, and approval of key economic, social and political organizations.

These approaches to effective execution of curriculum policy reflect strategies that the innovator can use to prepare for dealing with the problems of successful leadership: staying flexible and receptive to change and the innovations of others. They also point to several factors (some are identifiable in previous discussions) that can facilitate or constrain an innovation and its sustenance. The innovator and his or her team must not be deterred by failure. They should accept the fact that staff, particularly those who do not want to continue working in an organization are difficult to keep in an organization; there should be a tendency to back people and opportunities; reinvestment in the community of resources made out of using it should go straight back into it. There should be enthusiasm for change, which must be seen as a route to prosperity. People should be promoted on merit, not by any other criterion. The innovator and his team must be fascinated with the curriculum, not the money, as there is more to life than making money. Collaboration in various forms such as borrowing staff, sharing ideas, and favouring exchange does pay dividends. It is needless to waste time developing a product if someone else can do it better for you or with you, different types of organizations are good at different kinds of things, which gives a place better chance of survival. Success in almost all areas is possible as a result of either some liberalizing legislation or no legislation at all. There is need to be sensitive or being tuned to the environment in which an organization operates; and there should be cohesion: in other words, a strong sense of identity, and preventing change from tearing the organization apart. That these factors can be preeminent when applied to curriculum innovation in the context of the PHC/ Community health and cultural analysis common curriculum is clear from the chapters of this book.

Summary

To summarize this chapter on management of curriculum innovation and change in educational institutions for health professionals, one can use a model (Martin 1992) of four components that outline the process of executing change in organizations, which must be applicable to health educational institutions. The first component of the model is the rational-empirical which is a problem-solving approach that is logical, linear and sequential. The second component is specified as a social systems plan or attempt that gives much importance to the interpersonal and human inter-relationships of change. It emphasizes the significance of comprehending the meaning of change and the need to consult fully all interested groups in the organization and in the organization's sub-units. The third component is determined by the relative power to the opposing interest groups whom change relates to, and to a lesser extent by any collaborative or problem-solving approach to change. The fourth component (Martin calls it values-vision) incorporates desirability for new vision, on the basis of clear values. It provides a new perspective of purpose and commitment and may affirm a new or renewed mission and value base.

As Walt explains, the influence of the various actors will be significant subject to the aspect of change used. Professional or technical experts,

Francis Sarr

people with formal authority by virtue of their positions, and researchers will be most important in the rational-empirical model, where the major thrust is problem-solving. Communicators, representatives and skilled facilitators will employ the capability to co-operate and foster agreement in the social systems model. Negotiators and lobbyists will combine with those perceived to have power in the power-politics model. Finally, people with moral forces and a sense of commitment, people with charisma, and approved or new leaders will be the leaders of change in the value-vision model. Therefore, the implementation of innovation and change will to some degree additionally rest on the culture of the institution. As this and other chapters clearly demonstrate, cultural analysis views such political and policy processes as mainly open and democratic processes.

Final Points

To conclude, these points are outlined: one point is that the principles of PHC and community health remain valid today and attempts directed toward the achievement of the "Health for All" goal need to be intensified. However, the educational offerings that are designed to help make such a goal a reality require scrutiny. The rational and instrumental approach to planning the education of health professionals cannot adequately meet the educational needs of such professionals who must deal with a host of socio-cultural, economic, political and other factors which have affected and will continue to affect health care and related social systems in the years ahead. The cultural analysis approach to such curriculum planning that incorporates other useful educational planning principles, strategies and methods as proposed in this book will not only provide the necessary learning, it will also give the tools that teachers who are often overwhelmed by the requirement to orient curricula to the PHC approach need to be successful in meeting this demand. The cultural analysis approach includes the idea of a common curriculum that does not rest upon assumptions about cultural uniformity and consensus; quite the opposite- a common curriculum is a means of coping with cultural diversity in a positive way. Cultural analysis is a means by which those involved in the planning of curricula can choose from culture content that will equip all health professionals to comprehend and, if need be, to change the health systems in which they work in positive ways.

The second point, which is clearly contingent on the first point, is that like in the planning of curriculum content or coverage, an over-emphasis on the instrumental components of curriculum policy is a big gap that needs to be filled. The stress on the behavioural objectives approach to educational planning, and the related systems of examinations or testing, the use of forms of monitoring of standards, and one-way bureaucratic accountability, must shift to the health policy approaches described in the foregoing discussion. This will make teachers real professional educators, and the school manager and his or her staff (primarily) and others concerned controllers of the planning of the curriculum.

Thus, the approaches to school accounting that shifts the emphasis from tests or exams to the more open, comprehensive and flexible evaluation strategies like self-assessment schemes must translate into policy that is understandable and acceptable to all concerned, governments, funding agencies, teachers, communities, and other stakeholders.

The third point, therefore, is that a limited or simplified idea of the link between curriculum policyformulation and implementation produces another significant limitation that must be addressed. Implementation cannot be considered as part of a linear or sequential policy process in which political dialogue takes place during policy formulation, and implementation is undertaken by administrators or managers. The process is far from being simple and non-communicational, it is a complicated and interacting process which involves implementers of policy, who may actually influence the execution of policy and participate actively in the planning of innovation and change. To bring about the needed changes that will accommodate the realities of health care, policy-makers, training institutions, and professional associations should coordinate planned interdependent change in management systems, policies and resources including human resources. Clearly, this requires a change to a more open and participatory approach to innovation and change if curriculum policy is to find much expression beyond the drawing board. This should not mean that the linear and sequential problem-solving approach to implementing change must be rejected completely. The innovator may resort to using the rational-empirical approach in relating to especially health (and other) professionals, experts, researchers, etc, as this will be a necessary strategy in the change process. But as the evidence in the chapters of this book strongly demonstrates, the interacting and participatory approach to curriculum policy is most likely to produce the best results in most curriculum policy environments. Such an approach must rest on a clear understanding and use of effective policy analysis processes and techniques.

The foregoing chapters have demonstrated that the new realities of health care need new procedures, methods, strategies, techniques and processes of planning curriculum for the education of health professionals. They provide models, theories, and guidelines for understanding curriculum planning processes in the complicated health care environment, and how to make such processes yield the best results in particular situations. This book is an offering to teachers, policy makers, and others seeking to improve the education of health professionals for community health.

Bibliography

Aga Khan Foundation. (1988). Management Information system & Microcomputer in PHC. Geneva: Aga Khan Foundation.

Akiwumi, A. (1988). Setting a Standard for Basic Nursing Education in The West African Sub-Region.West African Journal of Nursing, March, 1088; 1 (1): 15-2….(1997). An Esthetic of Outrage. Newsweek. Washington: Newsweek, Inc, April 28

Barrett, O et al, ed. (1983). Approaches to Post-School Management. London: Harper & Row.

Barrows, H.S. (1997). The Problems and Responsibilities of Leadership in Educational Innovation. Network of Community-Oriented Educational Institutions for Health Sciences Newsletter. Maastricht: Network Publications, 27.

Bastien, J.W. (1994). Collaboration of Doctors and Nurses with Ethnomedical Practitioners. World Health Forum, Vol. 15, No 2.

Beattie, A. (1987). Making a Curriculum Work . In: Allen, P and Jolley, M, eds. Curriculum in Nursing Education. London: Croom Helm.

Ben-Eli, M.U. (2005/2006). Sustainability: the five core principles. Available at http://www. Sustainability labs.org/page/sustainability

Bensouda F. (1997). Autonomy-Freedom with Responsibility. In: proceedings of the Workshop on the New University of The Gambia, Kotu, December 12. Kanifing: University of the Gambia.

Bhatia, M., & Rifkin, S. (2010). A Renewed Focus on Primary Health Care: Revatilise or Reframe?. London: Department of Social Policy, London School of Hygiene and Tropical Medicine.

Bickford, D.T., Deborah J. B & David J. W. (2010?). Community: The Hidden Context for Learning. Dayton, USA: University of Dayton. Available at http://www.educause.edu. Accessed 20/6/2010.

Blair, M, Koury, S., De Witt, T., & Cundall, D. (2009). Teaching and training in community child health: learning from global experience. Available at http://ep.bmjjournals.com/content/94/4/123.extract.

Bloom B.S .(1956). Taxonomy of Educational Objectives. Handbook 1: The Cognitive Domain. New York: David Mckay Co Inc.

Boaden, N., & Bligh, J. (1999). Community-Based Medical Education. New York: Oxford University Press.

Boelen, C. (1995). Defining and Measuring the Social Accountability of Medical Schools. Geneva: WHO.

Bolam, R. (1982). School-Focused In-service Training. London: Heine-

Bibliography

mann Educational Books.

Bouhijjs, P.A.J. (1997). The Rijksuniversiteit Limburg, Maastricht, Netherlands: Development of Medical Education. In: Katz, F.M & Fulop, T., eds. Personnel for Health Care: Case Studies of Educational Programmes. Geneva: WHO.

Bourdieu, P. (1986). The forms of Capital. In Richardson, J (ed). Handbook of theory and research for the sociology of education, 241-256.

Boyer, E.L & Lee, D. M. (1996). Building Community: A New Future for Architecture Education and Practice. Princeton, N.J: The Carnegie Foundation for the Advancement of Teaching.

Bullock, M.E. (1983). The effects of humour on anxiety and divergent thinking in children. Dissertation Abstracts International [DA 8319150].

Cambell, S. (1996). Student Nurses in West Africa. Primary Health Care, TROPIX/BMCGATH, November, Vol. 6, No 10.

Cattell, R.E. (1949). The Dimensions of Culture Patterns by Factorization of National Characters. Abnormal Social Psychology, 44, 44369.

Cazov, E. (1983). Preventative Medicine: Problems of Specialization and Integration. World Health Forum, Vol.14, No. 3.

Center for Disease control and Prevention. (2011). What is health marketing ?. CDC 1600 Chfton Rd, Atlanta GA 30333, USA. Available at http://www. Cdc.gov/health communication /tools tem/

Chynoweth, P. (2006). The Built environment interdisciplinary: A theoretical model for decision-makers in research and teaching. Proceedings of the CIB working Commission, building education and research conference, Kowloon Sangri-la Hotel , Hong Kong, 10-13 April 2006

Cills Conference. (1998). Environment-Friendly Integrated Pest Management, September 1989, Banjul: Department of State for Agriculture.

Cohen, L.J. (1993). Discover the healing power of books. American Journal of Nursing, Medical Surgical Nursing, 10, 70 ± 74.

Coleman, J.S. (1988). Social capital in the creation of Human capital. American Journal of Sociology, Vol 94

Comite Pedagogique, The Institut Technologique De La Sante Public, Algeria. (1978). Preparing Health Personnel for Algeria.In: Katz, F.M & Fulop, T., eds. Personnel for Health Care: Case Studies of Educational Programmes. Geneva: WHO.

Comlan, A. A. (1985). Twenty Years of Political Struggle for Health. Brazzaville: WHO.

Cornbach, L.J. (1963). Evaluation for Course Improvement. In: Heath, R., ed. New Curricula. London: Harper and Row.

Cowley, R. (1991). The Challenge of World Health. Geneva: WHO.

C-Span Television. (1998). President Clinton's address to the Delaware Assembly, 8th May. USA: C-Span Television..... (1997). Daily Observer. Banjul: The Observer Company (Gambia) Ltd. November 12..... (1998).

Daily Observer. Banjul: The Observer Company (Gambia) Ltd. May 11. Dahlgren, G and Whitehead, M . (2006). European Strategies for tackling social inequities in health. Liverpool: University of Liverpool, WHO Collaborating Centre for Policy Research and Social Determinants of health. Dahlgren, G and Whitehead, M. (1991) Social Model of Health. Available at http://www.nwci.ie/download/pdf/determinants_health_diagram.pdf Davis, M.T. (2003). Outcomes –Based Education. Scotland: University of Dundee Centre for Medical Education Davis, G. (1998). Engaging Rural Communities in Educational Professions Studies: Unique Curriculum Development. Poster Presentation at the Network of Community-Oriented Education Institutions for Health Sciences Conference, Albuquerque, New Mexico, USA, October 17-22, 1998. Day, C. (1990). Places of the Soul. London: Harper Collins Publishers. De La Cuesta (1983) The Nursing Process: From Development to Implementation. Journal of Advanced Nursing, 1983; 8, 5:365-371. Department for the Environment, Food and Rural Affairs. (2009). Sustainable Growth. UK: Defra Department of Health. (2014). Primary and Community Health. Department of health, State Government of Victoria, Australia. Available at http://www.health.vic.gov.au/pch/ Department of Health & Social Welfare. (1998). Public Expenditure Review of the Health Sector. Banjul::MOH&SW. Dickinson, N. B. (1975). The head Teacher as Innovator: a Study of an English School District. In: Reid, W, et al, ed. Case Studies in Curriculum Change. London & Boston: Routledge & Kegan Paul. Drummond, D. (1987). Cited in Advisory Group on Health Technology Assessment Doc. (1991). Assessing The Effects of Health Technologies: Principles, Practice Proposals. London: Research and Development Department, London, UK: Ministry of Health. Durkheim, E. (1993). The Division of Labour in Society. New York: The Free Press.

Eisner, E. W. (1971). Confronting Curriculum Reform. Boston, Mass: Little, Brown. Enhancing Interdisciplinary Collaboration in Primary Health Care (EICP)

Bibliography

Initiative. (2004).Report of the National Primary Health Care Conference, Winnipeg, Manitoba, 2004.

Eraut, M. (1981). Accountability and Evaluation. In: Simon, B & Taylor W., ed. (1981). Education in the Eighties: the central issues. London: Batsford-- .(1997). An Esthetic of Outrage. News week. Washington: News week Inc, April 28.

Evlo, K., & Carrin, G. (1992). Finance for health care: part of a broad canvas. World Health Forum;13 (2-3):165-70.

Fonchingong, C.C and Fonjong, L.N. (2003). The concept of self-reliance in community development initiatives in the Cameroon Grassfields. Nordic Journal of African Studies 12 (2): 196-219

Foley, R.P., Polson, A.L & Vance, J.M. (1997). Review of the Literature on PBL in the Clinical Settings. Teaching and Learning in Medicine, 9, 4-9.

Fox-Rushby J. A. (1996). Costs Effects and Cost-effectiveness Analysis of a Mobile Maternal Health Care Service in West Kiang, The Gambia. Health Policy, 35, 123-143.

Further Education Curriculum Review and Development Unit. (1981). Vocational Preparation. In: Boyd-Barrett, O et al, ed.(1983). Approaches to Post-School Management. London: Harper & Row Publishers.

G 8 Summit. CNN Television, Cable News Network, Inc, Brirmingham, England, 7th May 1998.

Gadomski, A., Black, R., & Mosley, H .(1991). Constraints to the potential impact of child survival in developing countries . Health Policy and Planning, 5: 235-45.

Gagne, R. (1985). The conditions of Learning & Theoretical Instructions, 4th edn. New York: Holt, Rinehart and Winston.

Geertz, J. (1975). The Interpretation of Cultures. New York: Basic Books

Gilbert, J. (1981). Educational Handbook for Health personnel. Geneva: WHO.

Green, L.W., and Ottoson, J.M. (1999). Community and Population Health, 8th ed. New York and Toronto: WCB/McGraw-Hill.

Gofin, J & Gofin, R. (2005). Community-oriented primary care and primary health care. American Journal of Public Health, 95(5):757.

Goodland, R and Daly, H. (1996). Environmental sustainability: universal and non-negotiable. Ecological Applications, 6: 1002-1017.

Goodson, I. & Medway, P. (1975). The Feeling is Mutual. London: Times Educational Supplement, 1975.

Goodwin, P. (1998). Personal Interview on Gambian Culture, National Centre for Arts and Culture, July 1998.

Gordimer, N. (1998). Artful Words. Daily Observer. Banjul: The Observer Company (Gambia) Ltd, May 11, 1998.

Gorham, W.A. (1963). Methods for Measuring Staff Nursing Performance. Nursing Research, May-June, Vol. 12, No.1

Golladan, F.L. (1980). Comnity healthcare in developing countries. Finance Dev, September: 17(3):35-39

Graham, S. (1973). Studies of Behaviour Change in Public Health. American Journal of Public Health, Vol. 63, No 4.

Greeves, F. (1984). Nurse Education and the Curriculum. London & Sydney: Croom Helm.

Gross, N. (1971). Implementing Educational Innovations: A sociological Analysis of planned Educational change. N. York: Basic Books Inc.

Harden, R. (1998). Outcome-Based Education and Multiprofessional Learning. Paper presentation at The Network of Community-Oriented Educational Institutions for Health Sciences conference. New Mexico, USA, October 17-22, 1998.

Hardon, A.(1995). Applied Health Research. Amsterdam: CIP-Data Konkinklyke Bibiotheck, Den MS Hang.

Hirschfeld, M. (1997). Strengthening Nursing and Midwifery: A Global Study. Geneva: WHO.

Hirst, P. (1975). Knowledge and The Curriculum. London: Routledge and Kegan Paul.

Hoyle, E. (1972). Sociology of Education. British Journal of Educational Technology, Vol 3, Issue 2, May 1972

Hoyle, E. (1988). Micropolitics of Educational Organisations: Culture and Power in Education. Milton Keynes: Upon University Press.

Kindig, D and Stoddart, G. (2003). What is population health. Am J Public Health, March; 93(3):380-383.

Huckabay, L. M. (1963). Cognitive-Affective Consequences of Grading Versus Non-grading of Formative evaluations. Nursing Research, May-June, Vol. 28, No.3.

Hurst, K. (1985). Traditional versus Progressive Nurse Education: A Review of the Literature. Nurse Education Today, 5, p30-36.

Ignatiff, M. (1998). Daily Observer. Bakau: The Observer Company, April 16.

Infed. (2010). Curriculum theory and Practice. Available at http://

Bibliography

www.infed.org/biblio/b-curric.htm.

International Council of Nurses. (1989). Development of standards for Nursing Education and Practice. Geneva: ICN.

International Council of Nurses. (1986) .The Regulation of Nursing. Geneva: ICN.

International Fund for Agricultural Development (2011). A guide for project M&E, Section 3. Rome: IFAD

Jancloes, M. (1998) .The poorest of first: WHO activity to help the poor in greatest need. World Health Forum, Vol. 19, No3.

Jeguier, N. (1981). Appropriate Technology Needs Political Push. World Health Forum, Vol.2, No.4, p541.

Kahssay, H.M. (1998). Health Centres-The Future of Health Depends on Them. World Health Forum, Vol 12, No 2.

Katz, F.M & Fulop, T., eds. (1978). Personal for Health Care: Case Studies of Educational programmes. Geneva: WHO.

Kelly, A.V. (1982).The Curriculum. London: Harper & Row Publishers.

Kluckhohn, F & Stroctbeck, F.L. (1961). Variations in Value Orientations. Evanstone, III: Row, Peterson.

Kohlberg, L. (1964). Development of Moral Character and Moral Ideology. In: Hoffman, L.W, ed. Review of Child Development Research,Vol. I. Beverly Hills, Calif: Sage.

Kohlberg, L. (1989). Lawrence Kohlberg's Approach to Moral Education. New York: Columbia University Press.

Kuh, G.D. (2005). Student Success in College: Creating Conditions That Matter. San Francisco: Jossey-Bass.

Law, B. (1984). Uses and Abuses of Profiling. London: Harper & Row Publishers.

Lawton, D. (1983). Curriculum Studies and Educational Planning. London: Holder and Stoughton.

Leathard, A. (1997). Interpersonal Education and the Medical Profession: The changing Context in Britain. Education for Health. Abingdon, Oxfordshire: Carfax Publishing Ltd.

Lee, D. (1965). Enduring Human Values. In: Westby-Gibson, D. Social Perspectives on Education. New York: Wiley.

Levine, R., M. Rosenmoller and P. Khaleghian. (2001). Financial Sustainability of Childhood Immunisation: Issues and options. Global Alliance for Vaccines and Immunisations. Available at http://www, vaccinealliance.org/financing/identity.htn .

Lewis, S and Edwards, J. (2004). A thousand points of light?: moving forward on primary health care : a synthesis of the key themes and ideas from the national primary health care conference, Winnipeg, Manitoba, May 16-19, 2004. Available at http://books.google.gm/books/about/ A_Thousand_Points_of_Light.html?id=QSnRlgEACAAJ&redir_esc=y .

Linton, R, ed. (1940). Acculturation. New York: Appleton-Century-Crofts.

Locsin, A.C. (1981). The effect of music on the pain of selected post-operative patients. Journal of Advanced Nursing, 6,19-25 .

Loepp, F.L. (1999). Models of Curriculum Integration. Journal of Technology Studies, 25(2): 21-25.

Manning, G., Kent, C., and McMillen, S. (1996). Building community: the human side of work. Cincinnati, Ohio: Thomson Executives Press.

Marsenich, B. (1983). Teaching the steps of change. Training/HRD, March 1983.

Martin, E. (1992). Human service organizations: an American perspective. Social Policy and Administration, 26: 320-35.

McGuire, C.H. (1973). Diagnostic Examinations in Medical Education. Development of Educational Programmes for the Health Professions. Geneva: WHO.

McKenzie, J., Pinger, R and Kotechi, J.E .(2011). An Introduction to Community Health. Canada: Jones and Bartlett Publishers.

Megaghie, W,C . (1978). Competency-Based curriculum Development in Medical Education. Geneva: WHO.

Miles, M. (1975). Planned change and Organisational Health. In: A.Harris, A., Lawm., W, Mand & Prescott, W., eds. Curriculum Innovation. London: Groom Helm.

Miller, G.E .(1978). Educational Research and Development Centres for the Health Professions. Development of Educational Programmes for the Health Professions. Geneva: WHO.

Ministry of Health & Social Welfare .(1993). National Family Planning Policy. Banjul: MOH&SW.

Ministry of Health & Social Welfare. (1985). National PHC Review. Banjul: MOH&SW.

Ministry of Health & Social Welfare. (1994). National Health Policy 1994 -2000. Banjul: MOH &SW.

Ministry of Health & Social Welfare. (1998). Public Expenditure Review of the Health Sector. Banjul,: MOH&SW.

Bibliography

Ministry of Health. (1981). The Gambia Primary Health Care Strategy. Banjul: MOH.

Models and the Curriculum Process (2005). Available at . http:// furcs.flinders.edu.au/education/postgrad/clinicaled/HLED9005/oduleO1/ mod1-sec. elements elements

Module 1:The Curriculum in Clinical Education (2005). Available at http://furcs.flinders.edu.au/education/postgrad/clinicaled/HLED9005/ moduleO1/mod1-sec .

Monekosso, G.L . (1994). District Health Management. Brazzaville: WHO.

Monekosso, G.L. (1987). Evaluation of the strategy for Health for All by the year 2000. Brazzaville: WHO.

Monekosso, G.L. (1998). The Three Phase of Health Development Scenario. Brazzaville: WHO. ....(1997). Moving Strategy. London: The Economist News Paper Limited, 1998.

Mullan, F & Epstein, L.(2002). Community-oriented primary care: New relevance in a changing world. American Journal of Public Health, Vol. 92, No 11.

Murock, G.P. (1949) . Social Structure.New York: Macmillan,--(1996). News week. Washington: Newsweek Inc, September 30.

Oedipus Complex Archives.(1997). Available at: http:// vccslitonline.cc.va.us/oedipusthewreck/complex.htm.

Organisation for Economic Cooperation and Development. (2007). Human Capital: How what you know changes your life. OECD Insights. Available at http://www. Oecd.org/human capital howw

Palmer, M. (1962). Self Evaluation of Nursing Performance Based on Clinical Practice Objectives. Nursing Research, Vol. 12. No.1.

Parker, J.C & Rubin L, J. (1970). Process As Content: Curriculum Design and the Application of Knowledge. Chicago: Rand McNally & Company.

Parlett, M & Hamilton, D. (1972). Evaluation as Illumination. In: Tawney, D. (1976) Curriculum Evaluation Today. London: Macmillan.

Patton, M.Q. (1978). Utiliz ation-focused evaluation. Beverly Hills, CA: Sage.

Patton, M.Q. (1986). Practical Evaluation. Newbury Park: Sage.

Peters, K..E., Cristancho, S.M & Garces M. (2009). Closing the Gap in a Generation-Health Equity through Action on the Social Determinants of Health. Education for Health, 22(2):381.

Peters, R.S. (1966). Ethics and Education. London: Allen and Unwin.

Phenix, P.H. (1964). Realms of Meaning. London: McGraw-Hill.

Piaget, J. (1965). The moral judgment of the child. New York: The Free Press.

Plochg, T & Kalzinga, N.S. (2002). Community-based integrated care: myth or must? International Journal for Quality in Healthcare, 14:91-101.

Pratt, T (1998) Combating the Spirit of Fear. Daily Observer. Banjul: The Observer Company (Gambia) Ltd April 16.

Pfeffer, J and Salancik, G. (1978). The external control of organisations: A resource Dependence Perspectives. New York: Harper and Row Publishers.

Pfeffer, J. (1982). Organizations and Organization Theory. Boston: Pitman Publishing.--(2011). Problem-based learning (PBL) at learning theories.com. Available at http://www.learning theories.com/problem-based-pbl.html.

Putman, R.D. (1993). Making Democracy work. Princeton, N.Y: Princeton University Press.

Quenum C.A.A. (1985).Twenty years of Political Struggle for Health. Brazzaville: WHO.

Quinn, F.M. (1995). The Principles and Practice of Nurse Education. London: Chapman & Hill.

Raths, J.B. (1971). Teaching without Specific Objectives. Educational Leadership, April, pp 714-720.

Reid, T.R. (1997). Roman Empire. Washington: National Geographic Society.

Reynolds J, Skilbeck M. (1976). Culture and the classroom. London: Open Books.

Richards, R .(2000). What does "community-oriented" means any way?. Some thoughts on Zohair Nooman. Education for Health, Vol 15, No.2, 2002, 109-112.

Rifkin, S. (1986). Book. World Health Forum, Vol. 7, No.4.

Ritchie F. (1994). Education for PHC: Accommodating the New Realities. World Health Forum, Vol. 15, No.6.

Roper, N., Logan, W.W & Tierney, A.J .(1980). The Elements of Nursing. UK: Churchill Livingstone.

Rountree, D. (1981). Developing Courses for Students. London: MC Graw Hill Book Company (UK) Limited.

Rubin, H.R. (1998). Plenary session: status report - an investigation to determine whether the built environment affects parents' medical outcomes. Journal of Health Care Design, 10, 11 ± 13.

Ruderman, M (2000). Resource Guide to Concepts and Methods for community-based and collaborative problem-solving, Women's and Children's Health Policy Centre, Department of Population and Family Health Sciences, John Hopkins University School of Public Health. Available at http://www.jhsph.edu/research centre-and-institutes.

Sachs, J. (1979). Nature, Nurture and Growth. The Economist, June, 14th.

Saho, B. (1998). Material Culture and National Development. Daily Observer, Bakau: The Observer Company, May 5th.

Sapirie, S.A. (1998). WHO and Health Planning-the Past, the Present and the Future.World Health Forum. Geneva: Vol 9, No 3, p382-386.

Sarr, F. (1986). Assessing the Role of Evaluation in Maternal and Child Health in The Gambia. Research report submitted in partial fulfillment of the MSc in Public Health Degree, London University.

Schaay, N. & Sanders, D. (2008). International perspectives on PHC over the past 30 years. South Africa, Western Cape: University of the Western Cape, School of Public Health.

Schmidt, H.G., Neufeld, V.R., Nooman, Z.M. & Ogunbode, T. (1991). Introduction. Network of Community-Oriented Educational Institutions for Health Sciences . International Medical Education, Volume 66, No 5.

Schoberg, D. (2010).Teaching Tolerance. The Rotarian, Vol 189, No 2.

Schwirian, P.M. (1978). Evaluating the Performance of Nurses: A Multidimensional Approach. Nursing Research, Nov-Dec. Vol.12, No.6.

Scott- Peck, M.(1993). Meditations from the road. New York: Simon and Schuster.

Shah, A. (2013). Structural Adjustment-Amajor cause of poverty. Global Issues. Available at http://www. Global issues. Org/ article/ 3/structural-adjust.

Silayan-go, A. (1990). Entertainment for Health. World Health Forum Vol. 11, No3.

Skilbeck, M. (1976). Ideologies and Values, Unit 3 of Course E203. Curriculum Design and Development. Milton Keynes: Open University.

Sobral, D.T et al. (1978).The Medical School of the University of Brasilia.In: Katz, F.M & Fulop, T., eds. Personnel for Health Care: Case Studies of Educational Programmes. Geneva: WHO.--(1986). Social Science Research in a Changing World. World Health Forum, Vol. 16, No 15.

Socket, M. (?) .Towards a Professional Model of Teacher Accountability. In: R. McCormick (1982) Calling Education to Account. (Ed). UK: Heinemann Educational Books.

Socket, M. (?). Accountability: Purpose and Meaning. In: R. McCormick (1982) Calling Education to Account. (Ed). UK: Heinemann Educational Books.

Srinivasan, S., Fallon, L.R and Dearry, A. (2003). Creatng healthy communities, healthy homes and healthy people: Initiating a research agenda on the built environment and public health. Am J Public Health, September; 93 (9): 1446-1450.

Stenhouse, L. (1975). An Introduction of Curriculum Research and Development. London: Heinemann.

Stephenson, K.S., Richmond, S.A., Hinman, M.A & Christiansen, C.H. (2002). Changing Educational Paradigms to prepare Health Professionals for the 21st Century. Education for Health, Vol.15, No.1, 37-47.

Tenn, L., Sovaleni, R., Latu, R., Fotu, A et al. (1994). Getting the Community Involved in Developing a PHC Curriculum in Tonga. International Nursing Review, 41, 5.

Terris, M .(1983). The world Needs Schools of Public Health. World Health Forum, Vol. 4, No3, 216-218.

The Economist. (1997). Moving Strategy. London:The Economist Newspaper LTD, 1998.

The Free Dictionary. (2010). Available at: http:// encyclopedia2.thefreedictionary.com/Mande+Empire.

Thorndike , E. (1931). Human Learning. New York: Appleton Century Crofts.

Trueblood, L.A . (2000). Female genital mutilation: a discussion of international human rights instruments, cultural sovereignty and dominance theory. Colorado: Denver Journal of International Law and Policy, September 22.

Tyler, R.H. (1931). Basic Principles of Curriculum and Instruction. Chicago, III: University of Chicago Press.

Tylor, E.B. (1871). Primitive Culture. London: Murry.

UCL Institute of Health equity. (2010). Fair society, healthy lives: Strategic review of health inequalities in England post 2010 (the Marmot Review) Available at: http://www.instituteofhealthequity.org/projects/fair-society-healthy-lives-the-marmot-review

Ulrich, R.S. (1986a). Human responses to vegetation and landscapes. Landscape and Urban Planning, 13, 29 ± 44.

Ulrich, R.S. (1986b). Effects of hospital environments on patient well-being. Research report from Department of Psychiatry and behavioural medicine, Vol 9, No 55, University of Trondheim, Norway.

United Nations Conference on the Environment and Development. (1992). New York: UNCED.

UNESCO. (1999) . International Conference on the Human Genome. Windhoek, Namibia, 15-17 February, 1999: UNESCO.

UNICEF. (1997). Situation Analysis of Children & Women in The Gambia . (Draft Report) Banjul: Central Statistics Department.

United Nations. (2010). Ending Female Genital Mutilation. New York: UN Economic and Social Council, Commission on the Status of Women.

Vernon, H. (1998). Present Trents in Adult Education. Daily Observer. Bakau: The Observer Company Ltd, March 3.

Vernon, H. (1998). Teaching English as a Foreign Language. Daily Observer. Bakau: The Observer Company Ltd, March 31.

Walsh, W.J. (1978). The McMaster Programme of Education. In: Katz, F.M & Fulop, T., eds. Personnel for Health Care: Case Studies of Educational Programmes. Geneva: WHO.

Walt, G. (1994). Health Policy. London: Zed Books.

Watson, R . (1979). Do it, Be it, Live it". Newsweek. Washington: Newsweek Inc, October 6.

Wheeler, G. (1982).TheImplications and Process of Quality Control in Further and Higher Education. In: Wikstro¨m, B.M. (2000). Visual art dialogues with elderly persons: effects on perceived life situation. Journal of Nursing Management, 8, 31 ± 37.

Williams, R. (1976). Keywords. London: Collins/Fontana.

Wolf , K.N. (1999). Allied Health Professionals and Attitudes toward teamwork. Journal of Allied Health, 28, 15-20.

World Commission on the Environment and Development. (1987). Brundtland Report. New York: WCED.

Woodcraft, S. (2012). Social sustainability and New Communities: Moving from concept to practice in the UK. Procedia Behavoural and Social Sciences 68(2012): 29-42. Available at www. Science direct.com.

World Health Organisation. (2014). The World Health Report 2008- Primary Health Care (Now More then Ever). Geneva: WHO.

World Health Organization. (1978). Primary health care. Geneva: WHO.

World Health Organization . (1979). Primary Health Care. Geneva: WHO.

World Health Organization.(1987). Evaluation of the Strategy for Health-for-All by the year 2000 (7th Report). Brazzaville: WHO.

World Health Organization .(1995). Renewing The Health-for-All Strategy. Geneva: WHO.

World Health Organization. (1994). Equity, Solidarity and Health. Geneva: WHO.

World Health Organization. (1996). Evaluation of The Implementation of the global strategy for Health-For All by 2000, 1979-1976 (selected Reviews).Geneva: WHO.

World Health Organization. (2008). Primary Health Care, including Health Systems Strengthening: Report by the Secretariat. EB124/8, December 4, 2008.Geneva: WHO.

World Health Organisation.(2008). Closing the gap- WHO report on social determinants of health. Geneva: WHO Commission on Social Determinants of Health. Available at http://whqlibdoc.who.int/publications/2008/9789241563703_eng.pdf?ua=1

World Health Organization.(1973). Development of Educational Programmes for the Health Professional. Geneva: WHO.

World Health Organization.(1986). A Guide to Curriculum Review for Basic Nursing Education: Orientation to Primary Health Care and Community Health. Geneva: WHO.

World Health Organization.(1986). Regulatory Mechanisms for Nurse Training and Practice: Meeting Primary Health Care Needs. Geneva: WHO.

World Health Organization.(1989). Integration of Health Care Delivery. Geneva: WHO.

World Health Organization .(1995). Renewing the health-for-all strategy. Geneva: WHO.

Index

Printed in the United States
By Bookmasters